Po

P

written and researched by

ROB HUMPHREYS

Contents

<< STATUES ON THE CHARLES BRIDGE
< ART NOUVEAU SCULPTURE ON OBECNÍ DŮM

INTRODUCTION TO
PRAGUE

With some six hundred years of architecture virtually untouched by natural disaster or war, few other European capitals look quite as beautiful as Prague. Straddling the winding River Vltava, with a steep wooded hill to one side, the city retains much of its medieval layout and its rich mantle of Baroque, Rococo and Art Nouveau buildings have successfully escaped the vanities and excesses of modern redevelopment.

BUILDINGS ON THE OLD TOWN SQUARE

Best place for a view over the city

Prague is a city of red rooftops and golden spires, of wooded hills and stupendous views. Every visitor who climbs the steps to the castle is rewarded with a fantastic view over the city, but if you want to escape the crowds, check out some of the capital's other lofty vantage points.
SEE Letná > p.118, Petřín > p.54, Vyšehrad > p.110.

Physically, Prague may have weathered the twentieth century very well but it suffered in other ways. The city that produced the music of Dvořák and Smetana, the literature of Čapek and Kafka and modernist architecture to rival Bauhaus, was forced to endure a brutal Nazi occupation. Prague had always been a multiethnic city, with a large Jewish and German-speaking population – in the aftermath of the war, only the Czechs were left. Then for forty years, during the Communist period, the city lay hidden behind the Iron Curtain, seldom visited by Westerners. All that changed in the 1990s, and nowadays Prague is one of the most popular European city break destinations, with a highly developed tourist industry and a large expat population who,

if nothing else, help to boost the city's nightlife.

Prague is divided into two unequal halves by the river, which meanders through the heart of the capital and provides the city with one of its most enduring landmarks, the Charles Bridge. Built during the city's medieval golden age, this stone bridge, with its parade of Baroque statuary, still forms the chief link between the more central old town, or Staré Město, on the right bank, and Prague's hilltop castle on the left. The castle is a vast complex, which towers over the rest of the city and supplies the classic picture-postcard image of Prague. Spread across the slopes below the castle are the wonderful cobbled streets and secret walled gardens of Malá Strana, little changed in the two hundred years since Mozart walked them.

When to visit

Prague is very popular, which means that the streets around the main sights are jam-packed with tourists for much of the year. If you can, it's best to avoid the summer months, when temperatures soar above 30ºC, and you have to fight your way across the Charles Bridge. The best times to visit, in terms of weather, are May and September. The winter months can be very chilly in Prague, but if you don't mind the cold, the city does look good in the snow and the crowds are manageable. Christmas and New Year are perfect as there are Christmas markets right across town, and plenty of mulled wine and hot punch to keep you warm.

With a population of just one and a quarter million, Prague (Praha to the Czechs) is relatively small as capital cities go. It originally developed as four separate self-governing towns and a Jewish ghetto, whose individual identities and medieval street plans have been preserved, to a greater or lesser extent, to this day. Almost everything of any historical interest lies within these compact central districts, and despite the twisting matrix of streets, it's easy enough to find your way around between the major landmarks. If you do use public transport, you'll find an extensive and picturesque tram network and a futuristic Soviet-built metro system that rivals most German cities. With the Czech crown riding high and the country hoping to adopt the euro in the not too distant future, Prague is no longer the budget destination it once was. However, one thing you can be sure of is that the beer is better and cheaper than anywhere else in the EU.

VIEW OF THE CASTLE FROM THE CHARLES BRIDGE

PRAGUE AT A GLANCE

>>EATING

As in many cities, the main thoroughfares in Prague aren't the best places in which to find somewhere to eat and drink. One or two grand Habsburg-era cafés survive on the main junctions of the city centre, but for the most part the best cafés and restaurants are hidden away in the backstreets. There's a particularly acute dearth of decent places in and around Prague Castle and **Hradčany**, while expensive restaurants predominate in **Malá Strana**. For a much wider choice of cafés, and of cuisine, head to **Staré Město** and the streets of **Nové Město** just south of Národní.

>>DRINKING

Given that the Czechs top the world league table of beer consumption, it comes as little surprise to find that Prague is a drinker's paradise. Wherever you are in the city, you're never very far from a pub or bar where you can quench your thirst. **Staré Město** has the highest concentration of pubs and bars, but if you're looking for one of the city's new microbreweries or for a traditional Czech pub (**pivnice**), you'll need to explore the residential streets of **Nové Město**, **Vinohrady** or **Holešovice**. Look out, too, for the many alfresco drinking spots beside the river, on one of the islands, or in one of the city's many public parks.

>>NIGHTLIFE

Prague's often excellent theatre and concert venues are all very centrally located in **Staré Město** and **Nové Město**; the same is true for most small and medium-scale jazz and rock venues. **Žižkov** has more late-night pubs and bars than anywhere else, plus a smattering of gay and lesbian venues. One area that's up-and-coming for nightlife is **Holešovice**, in particular the old industrial and market area to the east of the metro line – the warehouse spaces here already house several of the city's newest clubs and venues. **Wenceslas Square** remains the traditional centre of Prague's seedier side.

>>SHOPPING

Pařížská, in Josefov, is home to the city's swankiest stores, among them branches of the international fashion houses. **Celetná** in Staré Město, and **Na příkopě** on the border of Nové Město, also specialize in luxury goods. The city's most modern department store is multistorey **My národní** on Národní. Czechs have had their own malls – known as **pasáže** – since the 1920s, and new ones continue to sprout up. The mother of all malls is **Palladium**, on náměstí Republiky, housed in a castellated former army barracks. For more off-beat, independent shops you need to explore the cobbled sidestreets of Staré Město and Nové Město.

OUR RECOMMENDATIONS FOR WHERE TO EAT, DRINK AND SHOP ARE LISTED AT THE END OF EACH PLACES CHAPTER

Day One in Prague

1 **Prague Castle** > p.32. From Hradčanské náměstí, the square outside the main castle gates, you get an incredible view over Prague.

2 **Cathedral of sv Vít** > p.32. Occupying centre stage in the castle's vast precincts is the city's Gothic cathedral.

3 **Old Royal Palace** > p.35. Visit the palace's vast, rib-vaulted Vladislav Hall.

4 **Golden Lane** > p.37. Built in the sixteenth century for the imperial guards, these tiny little cottages situated hard against the fortifications are now one of the most popular sights in the castle.

Lunch > p.39. *Villa Richter*, situated in the middle of the castle vineyards, has superb views across the rooftops and river to Staré Město.

5 **Church of sv Mikuláš** > p.47. This prominent Malá Strana landmark, below the castle, is Prague's most ornate Baroque church.

6 **Charles Bridge** > p.60. Prague's famous medieval stone bridge is packed with people and peppered with Baroque statues.

7 **Museum Kampa** > p.52.This art gallery houses a permanent collection of two Czech artists: Kupka, a pioneer in abstract art, and the cubist sculptor Gutfreund.

Dinner > p.57. Try the intimate French restaurant, *Café de Paris*, or for a more grandiose setting, head for the *Savoy* (right).

Day Two in Prague

1 Obecní dům > p.90. Book yourself on the morning tour round this cultural centre, an Art Nouveau jewel built in 1911.

2 Museum of Czech Cubism > p.70. Housed at the top of a Cubist house, with a Cubist café on the first floor and a Cubist shop on the ground floor.

3 Old Town Square > p.66. Prague's showpiece square, with its parade of Baroque facades, its giant statue of Jan Hus and its interactive astronomical clock.

4 Týn Church > p.68. This giant Gothic church's twin, unequal towers preside over Old Town Square.

🍴 Lunch > p.76. *Maitrea* is a smart, cave-like vegetarian restaurant near the Týn Church.

5 Pinkas Synagogue > p.80. Pay your respects to the 77,297 Czech Jews killed in the Holocaust, whose names cover the walls of this sixteenth-century synagogue.

6 Old Jewish Cemetery > p.81. An evocative medieval cemetery in which the crowded gravestones mirrored the cramped conditions in the ghetto.

7 Old-New Synagogue > p.79. This thirteenth-century synagogue is the oldest active synagogue in Europe and one of Prague's earliest Gothic buildings.

🍴 DInner > p.84. Sink into a wicker chair at *Le Café Colonial* (right) while tucking into one of their pasta dishes.

Communist Prague

Despite forty-odd years of Communism, the regime left very few physical traces on the city. However, if you know where to look there are several understated – and one or two ironic – memorials to the period.

1 Kinský Palace > p.68. It was from the balcony of this Baroque palace that Klement Gottwald proclaimed the 1948 Communist takeover.

2 Museum of Communism > p.89. It took an American expat to collect together the city's best collection of Communist memorabilia.

3 Jan Palach memorial > p.86. In 1969, two young men took their own lives in protest against the Soviet invasion of the previous year.

4 Národní třída > p.98. A simple bronze memorial commemorates the demonstration of November 17, 1989, which sparked the Velvet Revolution.

5 Memorial to the Victims of Communism > p.54. Olbram Zoubek's striking memorial at the floor of Petřín hill pays tribute to the thousands who were imprisoned, executed and went into exile.

6 Míčovna > p.39. Seek out the hammer and sickle added to this Renaissance building in the Royal Gardens by the Communist restorers.

7 Metronome, Letná > p.118. Take in the view from David Černý's metronome, which stands where the world's largest Stalin statue once stood.

8 Žižkov Hill > p.115. Once used as a Communist mausoleum, the Žižkov monument still boasts lashings of Socialist Realist decor.

9 Olšany cemeteries > p.114. Pay your respects to the Red Army soldiers who lost their lives liberating the city in May 1945.

Kids' Prague

Most kids will love Prague, with its hilly cobbled streets and trams, especially in summer when the place is alive with street performers and buskers. Prague Castle, with its fairytale ramparts and towers, rarely disappoints either.

1 Funicular
> p.55. The funicular at Újezd, which takes you effortlessly to the top of Petřín hill, is part of the public transport system and is a great way to start a day's sightseeing.

2 Petřín > p.54. The Mirror Maze is a guaranteed hit with kids of all ages, and if you need to wear them out even more, get them to walk up the mini-Eiffel Tower for top views.

3 Changing of the Guard > p.33. Prague Castle's armed guards are dressed like toy soldiers, and at noon every day they put on a bit of show to a melancholic modern melody.

4 Tram #22 > p.138. This tram takes you from Prague Castle, round a hairpin bend and across the river to Karlovo naměstí, a short walk from the PPS terminal.

5 Boat trip > p.138. From April to October, you can take a 45-minute boat ride from PPS terminal near Palackého most all the way to Troja, home of the zoo. > p.138.

6 Prague Zoo > p.124. Prague Zoo has had a lot of money spent on it, and it shows: modern enclosures, sensitive landscaping and everything from elephants to zebras.

Big sights

 **Old Town Square** The city's showpiece square, lined with exquisite Baroque facades and overlooked by the town hall's famous astronomical clock. **> p.66**

2 Charles Bridge
Decorated with extravagant ecclesiastical statues, this medieval stone bridge is the city's most enduring monument.
> p.60

3 Josefov
The former Jewish ghetto contains no fewer than six synagogues, a town hall and a remarkable medieval cemetery.
> p.78

4 Prague Castle
Towering over the city, the castle is the ultimate picture-postcard image of Prague. **> p.32**

5 Wenceslas Square The modern hub of Prague, this sloping boulevard was the scene of the 1989 Velvet Revolution. **> p.86**

Green Prague

1 Malá Strana terraced gardens Pretty little Baroque gardens laid out on the terraced slopes below the castle. **> p.50**

2 Vyšehrad This old Habsburg military fortress is now a great escape from the busy city. **> p.110**

3 Stromovka Large leafy park laid out between Výstaviště and the chateau of Troja. **> p.123**

4 Royal Gardens Prague Castle's formal gardens are famous for their disciplined crops of tulips. **> p.39**

5 Petřín This wooded hill on Prague's left bank provides a spectacular viewpoint over the city. **> p.54**

Baroque Prague

1 Loreto church A sumptuous Baroque pilgrimage complex with frescoed cloisters, a Black Madonna, and a stunning array of reliquaries and monstrances. > **p.43**

2 Old Town Square Probably the most impressive parade of Baroque facades and gables in all Prague. **> p.66**

3 Charles Bridge statues It's the (mostly) Baroque statues that make this medieval bridge so unforgettable. **> p.60**

4 Church of sv Mikuláš The city's finest Baroque church, whose dome and tower dominate the skyline of Malá Strana. **> p.47**

5 Strahov Monastery Strahov boasts two monastic libraries with fantastically ornate bookshelves and colourful frescoes. **> p.44**

Cafés

1 **Obecní dům** Café decor doesn't come better than this Art Nouveau masterpiece. **> p.93**

2 Montmartre Vaulted former haunt of the likes of Kafka, Werfel and Hašek. **> p.74**

3 Grand Café Orient Perfect reconstruction of a first-floor Cubist café from 1911. **> p.74**

4 Café Slavia Immortalized in a poem by Nobel Prize-winner Jaroslav Seifert, this café is haunted by the ghosts of generations of Czech writers. **> p.104**

5 Café Louvre First-floor café that roughly reproduces its illustrious 1902 predecessor. **> p.104**

Museums and galleries

1 **Veletržní Palace** The city's premier modern art museum is housed in the functionalist Trade Fair Palace. **> p.121**

2 Convent of St Agnes Gothic convent that provides the perfect setting for the national collection of medieval art. **> p.69**

3 UPM A treasure-trove of Czech applied art ranging from Meissen porcelain and Art Nouveau vases to avant-garde photography. **> p.82**

4 Museum Kampa Private collection housed in a converted watermill and stuffed with works by František Kupka, among others. **> p.52**

5 Museum of Czech Cubism Czech artists, sculptors and architects were at the forefront of the Cubist movement. **> p.70**

Art Nouveau Prague

1 **Praha hlavní nádraží** Fight your way through the subterranean modern station and you'll find Josef Fanta's glorious 1909 station more or less intact.
> p.87

2 Obecní dům Built in 1911 with the help of leading Czech artists, this is the city's finest Art Nouveau edifice. **> p.90**

3 Jan Hus Monument This gargantuan Art Nouveau monument forms the centrepiece of Old Town Square. **> p.67**

4 Grand Hotel Evropa A bit worn at the edges, the *Evropa's* café nevertheless retains its original 1905 decor. **> p.93**

5 Mucha Museum Dedicated to Alfons Mucha, the Czech artist best known for his Parisian posters. **> p.89**

Pubs

1 **U medvídků** One of the few central pubs to have changed little over the decades. > **p.76**

2 U kocoura Old-established Malá Strana pub serving Budvar. **> p.59**

4 U černého vola A truly authentic unpretentious pub serving Velkopopovický kozel beer. **> p.45**

3 Pivovarský dům Best of the city's new microbreweries with a good range of traditional pub food. **> p.106**

5 Letenský zámeček Great summer terrace overlooking the city and river from Letná. **> p.125**

Nightlife

1 Roxy City-centre dance club with its finger in all sorts of avant-garde pies.
> **p.77**

2 Mecca
This coolly converted factory is one of the most impressive, professional and popular clubs in Prague.
> p.125

3 Divadlo Archa
The most adventurous theatre in Prague, with everything from straight theatre to dance and live music.
> p.95

4 AghaRTA Jazz Centrum
Prague's best venue for jazz and blues is situated just off Old Town Square.
> p.77

5 Stavovské divadlo
The city's chief opera house has a glittering interior and many Mozart associations.
> p.77

29

Prague Castle

Prague's skyline is dominated by the vast hilltop complex of Prague Castle (Pražský hrad), which looks out over the city centre from the west bank of the River Vltava. There's been a royal seat here for over a millennium, and it continues to serve as headquarters of the Czech president, but the castle is also home to several of Prague's chief tourist attractions: the Gothic Cathedral of sv Vít, the late medieval Old Royal Palace, the diminutive and picturesque Golden Lane and numerous museums and galleries. The best thing about the place, though, is that the public are free to roam around the atmospheric courtyards and take in the views from the ramparts from early in the morning until late at night.

CATHEDRAL OF SV VÍT

Third courtyard ⓦ www.mekapha.cz.
March–Oct Mon–Sat 9am–5pm, Sun
noon–5pm; Nov–Feb closes 4pm. Free.
MAP P.34, POCKET MAP C11

Begun by Emperor Charles IV (1346–78), the **Cathedral** has a long and chequered history and wasn't finally completed until 1929. Once inside, it's difficult not to be impressed by the sheer height of the nave, and struck by the modern fixtures and fittings, especially the **stained-glass windows**, among them Alfons Mucha's superb

Cyril and Methodius window, in the third chapel in the north wall, and František Bílek's wooden altar, in the north aisle.

Of the cathedral's numerous side chapels, the grand **Chapel of sv Václav** (better known as Wenceslas, of "Good King" fame), by the south door, is easily the main attraction. The country's patron saint was killed by his pagan brother, Boleslav the Cruel, who later repented, converted, and apparently transferred his brother's remains to this

THE MAIN GATE

very spot. The chapel's gilded walls are inlaid with over a thousand semiprecious stones, set around ethereal fourteenth-century frescoes of the Passion; meanwhile the tragedy of Wenceslas unfolds above the cornice in sixteenth-century paintings.

The highlight of the ambulatory is the **Tomb of St John of Nepomuk**, a work of Baroque excess, sculpted in solid silver with free-flying angels holding up the heavy drapery of the baldachin. On the lid of the tomb, back-to-back with John himself, a cherub points to the martyr's severed tongue. Before you leave,

check out the Habsburgs' sixteenth-century marble **Imperial Mausoleum**, in the centre of the choir, surrounded by a fine Renaissance grille. Below lies the claustrophobic **Royal Crypt**, resting place of emperors Charles IV and Rudolf II, plus various other Czech kings and queens.

From noon, you can also climb the cathedral's **Great Tower** (daily: March–Oct noon–4.15pm; Nov–Feb noon–3.15pm), from the south aisle. Outside the cathedral, don't forget to clock the **Golden Gate**, above the south door, decorated with a remarkable fourteenth-century mosaic of the Last Judgement.

Visiting the castle

The castle precincts are open daily (April–Oct 5am–midnight; Nov–March 6am–11pm ☎ 224 373 368, ⊛ www.hrad.cz). There are two main types of **multi-entry ticket** available for the sights within the castle (excluding the cathedral). The **long tour** ticket (350Kč) gives you entry to most of the sights within the castle including the Old Royal Palace, the Basilica and Convent of sv Jiří, the Prague Castle Picture Gallery and Golden Lane. The **short tour** (250Kč) only covers the Old Royal Palace, the Basilica of sv Jiří, and Golden Lane. Castle tickets are valid for two days and are available from various ticket offices. Temporary exhibitions, such as those held in the Imperial Stables and Riding School, all have separate admission charges.

Most people **approach the castle** from Malostranská metro station by taking the steep shortcut up the Staré zámecké schody, which brings you into the castle from the rear entrance to the east. A better approach is down Valdštejnská, and then up the more stately Zámecké schody, where you can stop and admire the view, or up the cobbled street of Nerudova, before entering the castle via the main gates. From April to October, you might also consider coming up through Malá Strana's wonderful terraced gardens (see p.50), which are connected to the castle gardens. Alternatively, you can take tram #22 from Malostranská metro, which deposits you at the Pražský hrad stop outside the Royal Gardens to the north of the castle.

The hourly **Changing of the Guard** at the main gates is a fairly subdued affair, but every day at noon there's a much more elaborate parade, accompanied by a modern fanfare.

There are several cafés within Prague Castle at which you can grab a coffee and a snack, though you'd be far better off going outside the castle precincts.

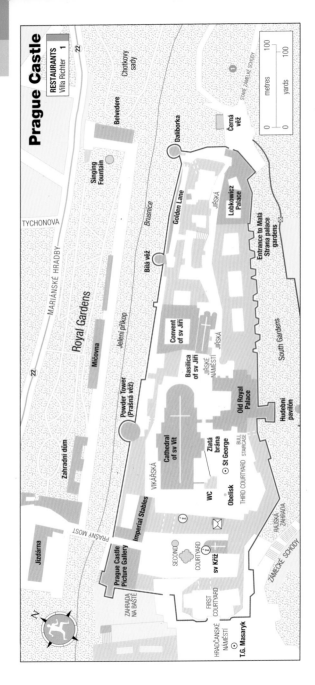

Prague Castle

RESTAURANTS
Villa Richter   **1**

Chotkovy sady

Belvedere

Singing Fountain

Daliborka

Černá věž

TYCHONOVA

MARIÁNSKÉ HRADBY

Royal Gardens

Míčovna

Jelení příkop

Brusnice

Golden Lane

JIŘSKÁ

Lobkowicz Palace

Bílá věž

Entrance to Malá Strana palace gardens

Convent of sv Jiří

South Gardens

Zahradní dům

22

Powder Tower (Prašná věž)

Basilica of sv Jiří

JIŘSKÁ

JIŘSKÉ NÁMĚSTÍ

Old Royal Palace

Hudební pavilón

Cathedral of sv Vít

VIKÁŘSKÁ

Zlatá brána

St George

BULL STAIRCASE

THIRD COURTYARD

Jízdárna

Imperial Stables

WC

Obelisk

RAJSKÁ ZAHRADA

PRAŠNÝ MOST

Prague Castle Picture Gallery

SECOND COURTYARD

sv Kříž

ZÁMECKÉ SCHODY

STARÉ ZÁMECKÉ SCHODY

ZAHRADA NA BAŠTE

FIRST COURTYARD

HRADČANSKÉ NÁMĚSTÍ

T.G. Masaryk

0   metres   100
0   yards   100

N

ALFONS MUCHA'S CYRIL AND METHODIUS WINDOW IN THE CATHEDRAL

OLD ROYAL PALACE (STARÝ KRÁLOVSKÝ PALÁC)

Third courtyard. Daily: April–Oct 9am–5pm; Nov–March 9am–4pm. 140Kč. MAP OPPOSITE, POCKET MAP C11

The **Old Royal Palace** is a sandwich of royal apartments, built one on top of the other by successive princes and kings of Bohemia, but left largely unused for the past three hundred years. It was in the **Vladislav Hall**, with its remarkable, sweeping rib-vaulting which forms floral patterns on the ceiling, that the early Bohemian kings were elected, and that every president since 1918 has been sworn into office. From a staircase in the southwest corner, you can climb up to the Bohemian Chancellery, scene of Prague's **second defenestration**, when two Catholic governors,

appointed by Ferdinand I, were thrown out of the window by a group of Protestant Bohemian noblemen in 1618. A quick canter down the Riders' Staircase will take you to the Gothic and Romanesque palace chambers containing **"The Story of Prague Castle"**, an interesting, if overlong, exhibition on the development of the castle through the centuries.

POWDER TOWER (PRAŠNÁ VĚŽ)

Vikářská. Daily: April–Oct 9am–6pm; Nov–March 9am–4pm. 140Kč. MAP OPPOSITE, POCKET MAP C10

The **Powder Tower** is where Rudolf's team of alchemists were put to work trying to discover the secret of the philosopher's stone. It now houses an exhibition on the history of the Castle Guard.

CHANGING OF THE GUARD

BASILICA OF SV JIŘÍ

Jiřské náměstí. Daily: April–Oct 9am–6pm; Nov–March 9am–4pm. MAP P.34, POCKET MAP C10–11

Don't be fooled by the basilica's russet-red Baroque facade; inside is Prague's most beautiful Romanesque building, meticulously scrubbed clean and restored to recreate something like the honey-coloured stone basilica that replaced the original tenth-century church in 1173. The double staircase to the chancel is a remarkably harmonious late Baroque addition and now provides a perfect stage for chamber music concerts. The choir vault contains a rare early thirteenth-century painting of the New Jerusalem from Revelation, while to the right of the chancel are sixteenth-century frescoes of the burial chapel of sv Ludmila, Bohemia's first Christian martyr and grandmother of St Wenceslas.

Good King Wenceslas

Disappointingly, there's very little substance to the story related in the nineteenth-century English Christmas carol, "Good King Wenceslas looked out". For a start, **Václav (Wenceslas)** was only a duke and never a king (though he did become a saint); he wasn't even that "good", except in comparison with the rest of his family; Prague's St Agnes fountain, by which "yonder peasant dwelt", wasn't built until the thirteenth century; and he was killed a good three months before the Feast of Stephen (Boxing Day) – the traditional day for giving to the poor, hence the narrative of the carol.

Born in 907, Václav inherited his title aged 13. His Christian grandmother, Ludmila, was appointed regent in preference to Drahomíra, his pagan mother, who subsequently had Ludmila murdered in 921. On coming of age in 925, Václav became duke in his own right and took a vow of celibacy, intent on promoting Christianity throughout the dukedom. Even so, the local Christians didn't take to him, and when he began making conciliatory overtures to the neighbouring Germans, they persuaded his pagan younger brother, Boleslav the Cruel, to do away with him. On September 20, 929, Václav was stabbed to death by Boleslav at the entrance to a church just outside Prague.

CONVENT OF SV JIŘÍ (JIŘSKÝ KLÁŠTER)

Jiřské náměstí ⓦ www.ngprague.cz. Daily 10am–6pm. 150Kč. MAP P.34, POCKET MAP C10

Founded in 973, Bohemia's earliest monastery was closed down in 1782, and now houses a large and slightly stodgy collection of **Czech nineteenth-century art**. The influential **Mánes** family provide some of the most accomplished works; more eye-catching, however, are the Balkan canvases of Jaroslav Čermák, the historical paintings of František Ženíšek and Mikuláš Aleš and the moody cityscapes of Jakob Schikaneder. Prize for most striking portrait goes to *Lady with a Greyhound*, by Václav Brožík.

GOLDEN LANE (ZLATÁ ULIČKA)

Daily: April–Oct 9am–6pm; Nov–March 9am–4pm. MAP P.34, POCKET MAP D10

A seemingly blind alley of brightly coloured miniature cottages, **Golden Lane** is by far the most popular sight in the castle, and during the day the whole street is crammed with sightseers. Originally built in the sixteenth century for the 24 members of Rudolf II's castle guard, the lane takes its name from the goldsmiths who followed a century later. By the nineteenth century, the whole street had become a kind of palace slum, attracting artists and craftsmen, its two most famous inhabitants being Nobel Prize-winning poet Jaroslav Seifert and Franz Kafka, who came here in the evenings to write short stories during the winter of 1916.

LOBKOWICZ PALACE (LOBKOVICKÝ PALÁC)

Jiřská 3 ⓦ www.lobkowiczevents.cz. Daily 10.30am–6pm. 275Kč. MAP P.34, POCKET MAP D10

Appropriated in 1939 and again in 1948 and only recently handed back, the Lobkowicz Palace now houses an impressive selection of the Lobkowicz family's prize possessions (with audioguide accompaniment), including original manuscripts by Mozart and Beethoven, old musical instruments, arms and armour and one or two masterpieces such as a Velázquez portrait, Pieter Brueghel the Elder's sublime *Haymaking* from the artist's famous cycle of seasons, and two views of London by Canaletto.

BASILICA OF SV JIŘÍ

SOUTH GARDENS (JIŽNÍ ZAHRADY)

Daily: April & Oct 10am–6pm; May & Sept 10am–7pm; June & July 10am–9pm; Aug 10am–8pm. Free. MAP P.34, POCKET MAP C11

These gardens, which link up with the terraced gardens of Malá Strana (see p.50), enjoy wonderful vistas over the city. Originally laid out in the sixteenth century, the gardens were remodelled in the 1920s with the addition of an observation terrace and colonnaded pavilion, below which is an earlier eighteenth-century *Hudební pavilón* (music pavilion). Two sandstone obelisks further east record the arrival of the two Catholic councillors after their 1618 defenestration from the Royal Palace (see p.35).

PRAGUE CASTLE PICTURE GALLERY (OBRAZÁRNA PRAŽSKÉHO HRADU)

Second courtyard ⓦ www.obrazarna-hradu .cz. Daily: April–Oct 9am–6pm; Nov–March 9am–4pm. 150Kč. MAP P.34, POCKET MAP C11

The remnants of the **imperial collection**, begun by Rudolf II, are housed here. Among the collection's finest paintings is Rubens' richly coloured *Assembly of the Gods at Olympus*, an illusionist triple portrait of Rudolf and his Habsburg predecessors that's typical of the sort of tricksy work that appealed to the emperor. Elsewhere, there's an early, very beautiful *Young Woman at Her Toilet* by Titian, and Tintoretto's *Flagellation of Christ*, a late work in which the artist makes very effective and dramatic use of light.

THE ROYAL GARDENS

FILIGREE IRONWORK AT THE BELVEDERE

ROYAL GARDENS (KRÁLOVSKÁ ZAHRADA)

Daily: April & Oct 10am–6pm; May & Sept 10am–7pm; June & July 10am–9pm; Aug 10am–8pm. Free. MAP P.34, POCKET MAP C10

Founded by Ferdinand I in 1530, the **Royal Gardens** are smartly maintained, with fully functioning fountains and immaculately cropped lawns. It's a popular spot, though more a place for admiring the azaleas and almond trees than lounging around on the grass. Set into the south terrace – from which there are unrivalled views over to the cathedral – is the Renaissance **ball-game court** (Míčovna), occasionally used for concerts and exhibitions. The walls are tattooed with sgraffito and feature a hammer and sickle to the side of one of the sandstone half-columns, thoughtfully added by restorers in the 1950s.

BELVEDERE (KRALOVSKÝ LETOHRÁDEK)

Mariánské hradby 1. Tues–Sun 10am–6pm. Free. MAP P.34, POCKET MAP D10

Prague's most celebrated Renaissance building is a delicately **arcaded summerhouse** topped by an inverted copper ship's hull, begun by Ferdinand I in 1538 for his wife, Anne (though she didn't live long enough to see it completed). The Belvedere's exterior walls are decorated by a series of lovely figural reliefs depicting scenes from mythology, while the interior is used for exhibitions by contemporary artists. In the palace's miniature formal garden is the so-called **Singing Fountain**, named for the musical sound the drops of water make when falling in the metal bowls below.

Restaurant

VILLA RICHTER

Staré zámecké schody 6 ☎ 257 219 079. Tues–Sun 10am–6pm. MAP P.34, POCKET MAP D10

Set amidst the castle vineyards, just outside the Black Tower (Černá věž), this place has three separate places one on top of the other: the *Piano Nobile* serves up classy fish, rabbit and wild boar dishes (600–700Kč); below, the *Piano Terra* specializes in Bohemian standards (150–300Kč); and *Panorama Pergola* is the perfect place to sample some Czech wines and soak up the view.

Hradčany

Hradčany – the district immediately outside Prague Castle – is replete with ostentatious Baroque palaces built on an ever-increasing scale. The monumental appearance of these palaces is a direct result of the great fire of 1541, which destroyed the small-scale medieval houses that once stood here and allowed the Habsburg nobility to transform Hradčany into the grand architectural showpiece it still is. Nowadays, despite the steady stream of tourists en route to the castle, it's also one of the most peaceful parts of central Prague, barely disturbed by the civil servants who work in the area's numerous ministries and embassies. The three top sights to head for are the Šternberg Palace, with its collection of Old Masters, the Baroque pilgrimage church of Loreto and the ornate libraries of the Strahov monastery.

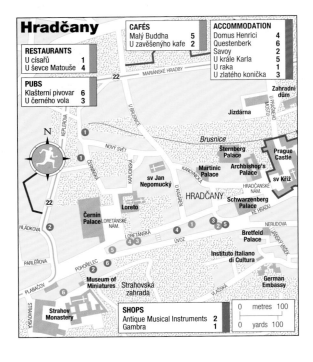

Hradčany

RESTAURANTS
U císařů	1
U ševce Matouše	4

PUBS
Klašterní pivovar	6
U černého vola	3

CAFÉS
Malý Buddha	5
U zavěšeného kafe	2

ACCOMMODATION
Domus Henrici	4
Questenberk	6
Savoy	2
U krále Karla	5
U raka	1
U zlatého koníčka	3

SHOPS
Antique Musical Instruments	2
Gambra	1

0 — metres — 100
0 — yards — 100

HRADČANSKÉ NÁMĚSTÍ

MAP OPPOSITE, POCKET MAP B11

Hradčanské náměstí fans out from the castle gates, surrounded by the oversized palaces of the old Catholic nobility. The one spot everyone heads for is the ramparts in the southeastern corner, which allow an unrivalled view over the red rooftops of Malá Strana, and beyond. Few people make use of the square's central green patch, which is heralded by a wonderful giant green wrought-iron lamppost from the 1860s and, behind it, a Baroque plague column. The most noteworthy palaces on the square are the **Schwarzenberg Palace**, at no. 2, with its over-the-top sgraffito decoration, and the sumptuous, vanilla-coloured Rococo **Archbishop's Palace**, opposite.

ŠTERNBERG PALACE

Hradčanské náměstí 15 ⓦ www.ngprague .cz. Tues–Sun 10am–6pm. 150Kč.

MAP OPPOSITE, POCKET MAP B11

This elegant early eighteenth-century palace is now an art gallery housing **European Old Masters** from the fourteenth to the eighteenth century. It's a modest collection, though the handful of masterpieces makes a visit here worthwhile, and there's an elegant courtyard café.

The highlights of the first floor include Dieric Bouts' *Lamentation*, a complex composition crowded with figures in medieval garb, two richly coloured Bronzino portraits, and Jan Gossaert's eye-catching *St Luke Drawing the Virgin*, an exercise in architectural geometry and perspective. Before you head upstairs though, don't miss the side room (11) containing Orthodox icons from Venice, the Balkans and Russia.

The second floor boasts a searching portrait of old age by Tintoretto, a wonderfully rugged portrait by Goya and a mesmerizing *Praying Christ* by El Greco. Be sure to admire the Čínský kabinet, a small oval chamber smothered in gaudy Baroque Chinoiserie, and one of the palace's few surviving slices of original decor. Elsewhere, there are a series of canvases by the Brueghel family, a Rembrandt and Rubens' colossal *Murder of St Thomas* (room 30).

The ground floor contains several superb Cranach canvases, plus one of the most celebrated paintings in the whole collection: the *Feast of the Rosary* by Albrecht Dürer, one of Rudolf II's most prized acquisitions, which he had transported on foot across the Alps to Prague.

SCHWARZENBERG PALACE

Hradčanské náměstí 2 🔊 www.ngprague
.cz. Tues–Sun 10am–6pm. 150Kč. MAP P.40,
POCKET MAP B11

The most outrageous, over-the-top, sgraffitoed pile on Hradčanské náměstí now houses a collection of **Czech Baroque art**, of only limited interest to the non-specialist. Chronologically, you should begin on the second floor, where you get a brief glimpse of the overtly sensual and erotic Mannerist paintings that prevailed during the reign of Rudolf II (1576–1612). The rest of the gallery is given over to the art that spearheaded the Counter-Reformation in the Czech Lands: paintings by the likes of Bohemia's Karel Škréta and Petr Brandl, and the gesticulating sandstone sculptures of Matthias Bernhard Braun and Ferdinand Maximilian Brokof.

MARTINIC PALACE

Hradčanské náměstí 8 🔊 www
.martinickypalac.cz. Daily 10am–6pm. 150Kč.
MAP P.40, POCKET MAP B11

Compared to the other palaces on the square, this is a fairly modest pile, built in 1620 by one of the councillors who survived the second defenestration (see p.35). Its rich sgraffito decoration, which continues in the inner courtyard, was only discovered during restoration work in the 1970s. On the facade, you can easily make out Potiphar's wife making a grab at a naked and unwilling Joseph. Guided tours of the interior are available, which along with a series of fine Renaissance ceilings, holds the **Museum of Mechanical Musical Instruments** (Muzeum hudebních strojů). It's an impressive collection ranging from café orchestrions and fairground barrel organs to early wax phonographs and portable gramophones. Best of all, though, is the fact that almost every exhibit is in working order – as the curators will demonstrate.

ČERNÍN PALACE

Loretánské náměstí 5. Closed to the public.
MAP P.40, POCKET MAP A11

Loretánské náměstí is dominated by the phenomenal 135-metre-long facade of the **Černín Palace**, decorated with thirty Palladian half-columns and supported by a row of diamond-pointed rustication. Begun in the 1660s, the building nearly bankrupted

ČERNÍN PALACE

future generations of Černíns, who were eventually forced to sell the palace to the Austrian state in 1851, which converted it into military barracks.

Since 1918, the palace has housed the **Ministry of Foreign Affairs**, and during World War II it was, for a while, the Nazi Reichsprotektor's residence. On March 10, 1948, it was the scene of Prague's third – and most widely mourned – defenestration. Only days after the Communist coup, **Jan Masaryk**, the only son of the founder of Czechoslovakia, and the last non-Communist in the cabinet, plunged to his death from the top-floor bathroom window of the palace. Whether it was suicide (he had been suffering from bouts of depression, partly induced by the country's political path) or murder will probably never be satisfactorily resolved, but for most people Masaryk's death cast a dark shadow over the newly established regime.

LORETO

Loretánské náměstí 7 ⓦ www.loreta.cz. Tues–Sun 9am–12.15pm & 1–4.30pm. 110Kč. MAP P.40, POCKET MAP A11

The outer casing of the Loreto church was built in the early part of the eighteenth century – all hot flourishes and Baroque twirls, topped by a bell tower that clanks out the hymn "We Greet Thee a Thousand Times" on its 27 Dutch bells. The focus of the pilgrimage complex is the **Santa Casa** (a mock-up of Mary's home in Nazareth), built in 1626 and smothered in a rich mantle of stucco depicting the building's miraculous transportation from the Holy Land. Pride of place within is given to a limewood statue of the Black Madonna and Child, encased in silver.

LORETO

Behind the Santa Casa, the much larger **Church of the Nativity** has a high cherub count, plenty of Baroque gilding and a lovely organ replete with music-making angels and putti. As in the church, most of the saints honoured in the **cloisters** are women. Without doubt, the weirdest of the lot is St Wilgefortis (Starosta in Czech), whose statue stands in the final chapel of the cloisters. Daughter of the king of Portugal, she was due to marry the king of Sicily, despite having taken a vow of virginity. God intervened and she grew a beard, whereupon the king of Sicily broke off the marriage and her father had her crucified. Wilgefortis thus became the patron saint of unhappily married women, and is depicted bearded on the cross (and easily mistaken for Christ in drag).

You can get some idea of the Loreto's serious financial backing in the church's **treasury**, whose master exhibit is a tasteless Viennese silver monstrance, studded with diamonds taken from the wedding dress of Countess Kolovrat, who made the Loreto sole heir to her fortune.

NOVÝ SVĚT

MAP P.40, POCKET MAP A11

Nestling in a shallow dip in the northwest corner of Hradčany, **Nový Svět** provides a glimpse of life on a totally different scale. Similar in many ways to the Golden Lane in the Hrad – but without the crowds – this picturesque cluster of brightly coloured cottages is all that's left of Hradčany's medieval slums, painted up and sanitized in the eighteenth and nineteenth centuries.

STRAHOV MONASTERY

Strahovské nadvoří 1 ⓦ www
.strahovmonastery.cz. Libraries: daily 9am–noon
& 1–5pm, 80Kč. Gallery: daily 9am–noon &
12.30–5pm, 60Kč. MAP P.40, POCKET MAP A12

The Baroque entrance to the Strahov monastery is topped by a statue of St Norbert, who founded the order in 1140 and whose relics were brought here in 1627. The church, which was remodelled in Baroque times, is well worth a peek for its colourful frescoes relating to St Norbert's life, but it's the monastery's two ornate Baroque **libraries** (*knihovny*) that are the real reason for visiting Strahov.

The **Philosophical Hall** has walnut bookcases so tall they almost touch the frescoes on the library's lofty ceiling, while the paintings on the low-ceilinged

Theological Hall are framed by wedding-cake-style stuccowork. Look out, too, for the collection of curios in the glass cabinets outside the library, which features shells, turtles, crabs, lobsters, dried-up sea monsters, butterflies, beetles and plastic fruit. There's even a pair of whales' penises displayed alongside a narwhal horn, harpoons and a model ship.

The monastery's collection of religious art, displayed in the **Strahov Gallery** (*obrazárna*) above the cloisters, contains one or two gems: a portrait of Emperor Rudolf II by his court painter, Hans von Aachen, plus a superb portrait of Rembrandt's elderly mother by Gerrit Dou.

MUSEUM OF MINIATURES

Strahovské nadvoří 11 ⓦ www
.muzeumminiatur.com. Daily 9am–5pm. 50Kč.
MAP P.40, POCKET MAP A12

This small museum displays forty or so works by the Russian **Anatoly Konyenko**, including the smallest book in the world, a thirty-page edition of Chekhov's *Chameleon*. Among the other miracles of miniature manufacture are a flea bearing golden horseshoes, scissors, and a key and lock; the Lord's Prayer written on a human hair; and a caravan of camels passing through the eye of a needle.

STRAHOV MONASTERY

Shops

ANTIQUE MUSIC INSTRUMENTS

Pohořelec 7 & 9. Daily 9am–6pm. MAP P.40. POCKET MAP A12

More than just lutes and old violins, this place also sells icons, Art Nouveau glass, clocks and model trains and cars.

GAMBRA

Černínská 5. March–Oct Wed–Sun noon–5.30pm; Nov–Feb Sat & Sun noon–5.30pm. MAP P.40. POCKET MAP A11

The commercial gallery of Prague's small but dogged Surrealist movement, past and present, is a dedicated promoter of the works of the late animator extraordinaire, Jan Švankmajer, and his wife, the artist Eva Švankmajerová, who lives nearby.

Cafés

MALÝ BUDDHA

Úvoz 46. Tues–Sun 1–10.30pm. MAP P.40. POCKET MAP A12

Typical Prague teahouse decor, with a Buddhist altar in one corner and good vegetarian Vietnamese snacks on the menu. A very useful smoke-free Hradčany haven.

MALÝ BUDDHA

U ZAVĚŠENÝHO KAFE (THE HANGING CAFÉ)

Úvoz 6. Daily 11am–midnight. MAP P.40. POCKET MAP B11

A pleasant, smoky crossover café/pub serving cheap beer and traditional Czech food in a handy spot near the Hrad.

Restaurants

U CÍSAŘŮ (THE EMPEROR)

Loretánská 5 ☎ 220 518 484. Daily 9am–1am. MAP P.40. POCKET MAP B11

Upmarket medieval place serving up hearty, meaty Czech dishes, as well as trout, butterfish and fondue for 400Kč and upwards.

U ŠEVCE MATOUŠE (THE COBBLER MATOUŠ)

Loretánské náměstí 4 ☎ 220 514 536. Daily 11am–4pm & 6–11pm. MAP P.40. POCKET MAP A11

Large steak and chips (300Kč), is the speciality of this former cobbler's, which is one of the few half-decent places to eat in the castle district.

Pubs

KLAŠTERNÍ PIVOVAR (THE MONASTERY BREWERY)

Strahovské nádvoří 1. Daily 10am–11pm. MAP P.40. POCKET MAP A12

Tourist-friendly monastic brewery, offering their own light and dark St Norbert beers and Czech pub food.

U ČERNÉHO VOLA (THE BLACK OX)

Loretánské náměstí 1. Daily 10am–10pm. MAP P.40. POCKET MAP A11

Great traditional Prague pub doing a brisk business serving huge quantities of popular light beer Velkopopovický kozel to thirsty local workers, soaked up with a few classic pub snacks.

Malá Strana

Malá Strana, Prague's picturesque "Little Quarter", sits below the castle and is in many ways the city's most entrancing area. Its many peaceful, often hilly, cobbled backstreets have changed very little since Mozart walked them during his frequent visits to Prague between 1787 and 1791. They conceal a whole host of quiet terraced gardens, as well as the wooded Petřín Hill, which together provide the perfect inner-city escape in the summer months. The Church of sv Mikuláš, by far the finest Baroque church in Prague, and the Museum Kampa, with its unrivalled collection of works by František Kupka, are the two major sights.

MALOSTRANSKÉ NÁMĚSTÍ

MAP P.48–49, POCKET MAP D11

Malostranské náměstí, Malá Strana's arcaded main square, is dominated and divided in two by the Baroque church of sv Mikuláš (see opposite). Trams and cars wind their way across the cobbles below the church, regularly dodged by a procession of people heading up the hill to the castle. On the square's north side at no. 18, distinguished by its two little turrets and rather shocking pistachio and vanilla colour scheme, is the **dům Smiřických**, where, in 1618, the Protestant posse met to decide how to get rid of Emperor Ferdinand's Catholic councillors: whether to attack them with daggers, or, as they eventually attempted, to kill them by chucking them out of the window (see p.35) of the Old Royal Palace.

PARLIAMENT

Sněmovna 4 ⓦ www.psp.cz. MAP P.48–49, POCKET MAP D11

The Czech parliament occupies a Neoclassical palace that served as the provincial Diet in the nineteenth century. Later it housed the National Assembly of the First Republic in 1918, the Czech National Council after federalization in 1968, and, since 1993, as home to the **Chamber of Deputies** (Poslanecká sněmovna), the (more important) lower house of the Czech parliament. To find out more, visit the **information centre** at Malostranské náměstí 6 (Mon–Fri 9am–4pm).

HOUSE SIGN ON NERUDOVA

CHURCH OF SV MIKULÁŠ

Malostranské náměstí ⓦ www.psalterium
.cz. Daily: March–Oct 9am–5pm; Nov–Feb
9am–4pm. 70Kč. MAP P.48–49, POCKET MAP C11–D12

Towering over the whole of
Malá Strana is the Baroque
church of **sv Mikuláš** (St
Nicholas), whose giant green
dome and tower are among the
most characteristic landmarks
on Prague's left bank. Built
by the Jesuits in the early
eighteenth century, it was their
most ambitious project yet
in Bohemia, and the ultimate
symbol of their stranglehold
on the country. Nothing
about the relatively plain west
facade prepares you for the
overwhelming High Baroque
interior. The vast fresco in the
nave portrays some of the more
fanciful miraculous feats of
St Nicholas, while the dome at
the east end of the church is
even more impressive, thanks,
more than anything, to its sheer
height. Leering over you as you
gaze up at the dome are four
terrifyingly oversized and stern
Church Fathers, one of whom
brandishes a gilded thunderbolt,
leaving no doubt as to the
gravity of the Jesuit message. It's
also possible to climb the **tower**

(daily: April–Oct 10am–7pm;
Nov–March 10am–6pm) for
fine views over Malá Strana and
the Charles Bridge.

NERUDOVA

MAP P.48–49, POCKET MAP C11

The busiest of the cobbled
streets leading up to the castle
is **Nerudova**. Historically,
this was the city's main area
for craftsmen, artisans and
artists, though the shops and
restaurants that line Nerudova
now are mostly predictably and
shamelessly aimed at tourists
heading for the castle. Many
of the houses that line the
street retain their medieval
barn doors and peculiar
pictorial house signs. One of
Nerudova's fancier buildings,
at no. 5, is the **Morzin Palace**,
now the Romanian Embassy,
its doorway supported by two
Moors (a pun on the owner's
name). Meanwhile, opposite,
two giant eagles hold up the
portal of the **Thun-Hohenštejn
Palace**, now the Italian
Embassy. Further up the street,
according to legend, Casanova
and Mozart are said to have
met up at a ball given by the
aristocrat owners of no. 33, the
Bretfeld Palace.

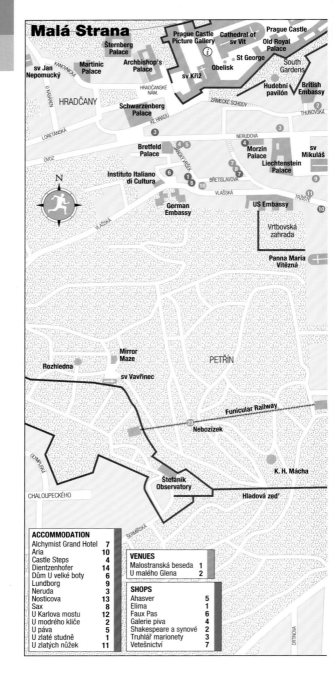

Malá Strana

ACCOMMODATION
Alchymist Grand Hotel	7
Aria	10
Castle Steps	4
Dientzenhofer	14
Dům U velké boty	6
Lundborg	9
Neruda	3
Nosticova	13
Sax	8
U Karlova mostu	12
U modrého klíče	2
U páva	5
U zlaté studně	1
U zlatých nůžek	11

VENUES
Malostranská beseda	1
U malého Glena	2

SHOPS
Ahasver	5
Elima	1
Faux Pas	6
Galerie piva	4
Shakespeare a synové	2
Truhlář marionety	3
Vetešnictví	7

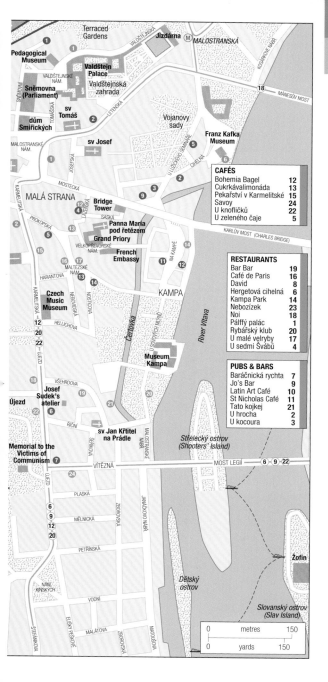

CAFÉS

Bohemia Bagel	12
Cukrkávalimonáda	13
Pekařství v Karmelitské	15
Savoy	24
U knoflíčků	22
U zeleného čaje	5

RESTAURANTS

Bar Bar	19
Café de Paris	16
David	8
Hergetová cihelná	6
Kampa Park	14
Nebozízek	23
Noi	18
PáLffý palác	1
Rybářský klub	20
U malé velryby	17
U sedmi Švábů	4

PUBS & BARS

Baráčnická rychta	7
Jo's Bar	9
Latin Art Café	10
St Nicholas Café	11
Tato kojkej	21
U hrocha	2
U kocoura	3

49

VALDŠTEJN PALACE

Valdštejnské náměstí 4 ⓦ www.senat.cz.
Tours Sat & Sun: April–Sept 10am–5pm;
Oct–March 10am–4pm. Free. MAP P.48–49,
POCKET MAP D11

Built in the 1620s for **Albrecht
von Waldstein**, commander of
the Imperial Catholic armies
of the Thirty Years' War, the
Valdštejn Palace was one of
the first and largest Baroque
palaces in the city. Nowadays, it
houses the Czech parliament's
upper house, or **Senate (Senát)**,
whose sumptuous Baroque
chambers can be visited on a
guided tour at weekends.

PEDAGOGICAL MUSEUM

Valdštejnská 20 ⓦ www.pmjak.cz. Tues–Sun
10am–12.30pm & 1–5pm 60Kč. MAP P.48–49,
POCKET MAP D11

The **Pedagogical Museum**
occupies a palace opposite
the Czech Senate, and houses
a permanent exhibition on
the history of education in
the Czech Lands. Despite
being recently revamped, the
museum is a fairly dry affair,
although you do get to learn
about the Czech teacher **Jan
Amos Komenský** (1592–1670)
– known in English as John
Comenius. An early advocate
of universal education,
Komenský's methods are taken
for granted now, but were
revolutionary for their time.

VALDŠTEJNSKÁ ZAHRADA (PALACE GARDENS)

April–Oct daily 10am–6pm. Free. MAP P.48–49,
POCKET MAP D11

Valdštejn Palace's **formal
gardens** are accessible from
the palace's main entrance, and
also from a doorway in the
palace walls along Letenská.
The gardens' focus is a gigantic
Italianate **sala terrena**, a
monumental loggia decorated
with frescoes of the Trojan
Wars, which stands at the end
of an avenue of sculptures. In
addition, there are a number
of peacocks, a pseudo grotto
along the south wall, with
quasi-stalactites, and an aviary
of eagle owls.

TERRACED PALACE GARDENS

Valdštejnská. Daily: April & Oct 9am–6pm;
May & Sept 9am–7pm; June & July
9am–9pm, Aug 9am–8pm. 80Kč.
MAP P.48–49, POCKET MAP D10

A great way to reach the Castle
is via Malá Strana's Baroque
terraced gardens, on the
steep slopes where the royal
vineyards used to be. Dotted
with urns and statuary, they
command superb views over
Prague. From Valdštejnská,
you enter via the Ledeburská
zahrada, gardens which
eventually connect higher up
with the castle's own South
Gardens (see p.38).

THE SALA TERRENA IN THE VALDŠTEJN PALACE'S GARDENS

FRANZ KAFKA MUSEUM

Cihelná 2b ⓦ www.kafkamuseum.cz. Daily 10am–6pm. 120Kč. MAP P.48–49, POCKET MAP E11

This museum offers a fairly sophisticated rundown of the life and works of the Czech–German writer **Franz Kafka** (1883–1924). The first section includes photos of the old ghetto into which Kafka was born, an invoice from his father's shop, with the logo of a jackdaw (*kavka* in Czech), copies of his job applications, requests for sick leave, one of his reports on accident prevention in the workplace, and facsimiles of his pen sketches. Upstairs, audiovisuals and theatrical trickery are used to explore the torment, alienation and claustrophobia Kafka felt throughout his life and expressed in his writings. On a lighter note, don't miss David Černý's **Pissing Figures** (Čůrající postavy) statue in the courtyard outside, which features two men urinating into a pool shaped like the Czech Republic.

PISSING FIGURES BY DAVID ČERNÝV

MALTÉZSKÉ NÁMĚSTÍ

MAP P.48–49, POCKET MAP D12

Maltézské náměstí is one of a number of delightful little squares between Karmelitská and the river. At the north end is a plague column, topped by a statue of St John the Baptist, but the square takes its name from the Order of the Knights of St John of Jerusalem (now known as the Maltese Knights), who in 1160 founded the nearby church of **Panna Maria pod řetězem** (St Mary below-the-chain), so called because it was the Knights' job to guard the Judith Bridge (predecessor to the Charles Bridge). Only two bulky Gothic towers are still standing and the apse is now thoroughly Baroque, but the nave remains unfinished and open to the elements.

JOHN LENNON WALL

MAP P.48–49, POCKET MAP D12

The pretty little square of **Velkopřevorské náměstí** echoes to the sound of music from the nearby Prague conservatoire, its northern limit marked by the garden wall of the Grand Priory of the Maltese Knights. Here, following John Lennon's death in 1980, Prague's youth established an ad hoc shrine smothered in graffiti tributes to the ex-Beatle. The running battle between police and graffiti artists continued well into the 1990s, with the society of Maltese Knights taking an equally dim view of the mural, but a compromise has now been reached and the wall's scribblings legalized. While you're in the vicinity, be sure to check out the love padlocks which have been secured to the railings of the nearby bridge.

KAMPA

MAP P.48–49, POCKET MAP E12–D13

Heading for **Kampa**, the largest of the Vltava's islands, with its cafés, old mills and serene riverside park, is the perfect way to escape the crowds. The island is separated from the left bank by Prague's "Little Venice", a thin strip of water called **Čertovka** (Devil's Stream), which used to power several mill-wheels until the last one ceased to function in 1936. For much of its history, the island was the city's main wash-house area, a fact commemorated by the church of **sv Jan Křtitel na Prádle** (St John-the-Baptist at the Cleaners) on Říční. It wasn't until the sixteenth and seventeenth centuries that the Nostitz family, who owned Kampa, began to develop the northern half of the island; the southern half was left untouched, and today is laid out as a public park, with riverside views across to Staré Město. To the north, the oval main square, **Na Kampě**, once a pottery market, is studded with slender acacia trees and cut through by the Charles Bridge, to which it is connected by a double flight of steps.

MUSEUM KAMPA

U Sovových mlýnů 2 ⓦ www.museumkampa.cz. Daily 10am–6pm. 160Kč. MAP P.48–49, POCKET MAP D13–E13

Housed in an old riverside watermill, **Museum Kampa** is dedicated to the private art collection of Jan and Meda Mládek. As well as temporary exhibitions, the stylish modern gallery also houses the best of the Mládeks' collection, including a whole series of works by the Czech artist **František Kupka**, seen by many as the father of abstract art. These range from early Expressionist watercolours to transitional pastels like *Fauvist Chair* from 1910, and more abstract works, such as the seminal oil painting, *Cathedral and Study for Fugue in Two Colours*, from around 1912. The gallery also displays a good selection of Cubist and later interwar works by the sculptor **Otto Gutfreund** and a few collages by postwar surrealist Jiří Kolář.

VRTBOVSKÁ ZAHRADA

Karmelitská 25 ⓦ www.vrtbovska.cz. April–Oct daily 10am–6pm. 55Kč. MAP P.48–49, POCKET MAP C12

One of the most elusive of Malá Strana's many Baroque gardens, the **Vrtbovská zahrada** was founded on the site of the former vineyards of the Vrtbov Palace. Laid out on Tuscan-style terraces, dotted with ornamental urns and statues of the gods by Matthias Bernhard Braun, the gardens twist their way up the lower slopes of Petřín Hill to an observation terrace from where there's a spectacular rooftop perspective on the city.

VIEW OF KAMPA FROM THE CHARLES BRIDGE

PANNA MARIA VÍTĚZNÁ

CHURCH OF PANNA MARIA VÍTĚZNÁ

Karmelitská 9 ⓦ www.pragjesu.com.
Mon–Sat 8.30am–7pm, Sun 8.30am–8pm.
Free. MAP P.48–49, POCKET MAP C12–D12

Surprisingly, given its rather plain exterior, the church of **Panna Maria Vítězná** (St Mary the Victorious) houses a high-kitsch wax effigy of the infant Jesus as a precocious 3-year-old, enthroned in a glass case. Attributed with miraculous powers, this image, known as the **Bambino di Praga** (or Prazské Jezulátko), became an object of international pilgrimage and continues to attract visitors. The *bambino* boasts a vast personal wardrobe of expensive swaddling clothes – approaching a hundred separate outfits at the last count – regularly changed by the Carmelite nuns. Some of these outfits are on display in a small museum, up the spiral staircase in the south aisle, including a selection of his velvet and satin overgarments sent from all over the world.

CZECH MUSIC MUSEUM

Karmelitská 2 ⓦ www.nm.cz. Mon 1–6pm, Wed 10am–8pm, Thurs, Sat & Sun 10am–6pm, Fri 9am–6pm. 100Kč. MAP P.48–49, POCKET MAP D12–13

Housed in a former nunnery, the permanent collection of the **Czech Music Museum** (České muzeum hudby) begins with a crazy cut-and-splice medley of musical film footage from the last century. Next up is August Förster's pioneering quarter-tone grand piano from 1924 – you can even listen to Alois Hába's microtonal *Fantazie no. 10* composed for, and performed on, its three keyboards. After this rather promising start, the museum settles down into a conventional display of old central European instruments, from a precious Baumgartner clavichord and an Amati violin to Neapolitan mandolins and a vast contrabass over 2m in height. Best of all is the fact that you can hear many of the instruments on display being put through their paces at listening posts in each room.

JOSEF SUDEK'S ATELIER

Újezd 30 ⓦ www.sudek-atelier.cz. Wed–Sun 10am–6pm. 10Kč. MAP P.48–49, POCKET MAP D13

Hidden behind the buildings on the east side of the Újezd is a faithful reconstruction of the cute little wooden garden studio, where **Josef Sudek** (1896–1976), the great Czech photographer, lived with his sister from 1927. Sudek moved out in 1958, but he used the place as his darkroom to the end of his life. The twisted tree in the front garden will be familiar to those acquainted with the numerous photographic cycles he based around the studio. The building has only a few of Sudek's personal effects and is now used for temporary exhibitions of other photographers' works.

MEMORIAL TO THE VICTIMS OF COMMUNISM

Újezd/Vítězná. MAP P.48–49, POCKET MAP D14

In 2002, the Czechs finally erected a **Memorial to the Victims of Communism**. The location has no particular resonance with the period, but the memorial itself has an eerie quality, especially when illuminated at night. It consists of a series of statues, self-portraits by sculptor **Olbram Zoubek**, standing on steps leading down from Petřín hill behind, each in varying stages of disintegration. The inscription at the base of the monument reads "205,486 convicted, 248 executed, 4500 died in prison, 327 annihilated at the border, 170,938 emigrated".

PETŘÍN

MAP P.48–49, POCKET MAP A13–C13

The hilly wooded slopes of **Petřín**, distinguished by the Rozhledna, a scaled-down version of the Eiffel Tower, make up the largest green space in the city centre. The tower is just one of several exhibits which survive from the **1891 Prague Exhibition**, whose modest legacy also includes the hill's funicular railway (see opposite). At the top of the hill, it's possible to trace the southernmost perimeter wall of the old city, popularly known as the **Hunger Wall**

MEMORIAL TO THE VICTIMS OF COMMUNISM

THE FUNICULAR RAILWAY

ŠTEFÁNIK OBSERVATORY

Ⓦ www.observatory.cz. Tues–Sun, times vary.
60Kč. MAP P.48–49, POCKET MAP B14–C14

At the top of the hill, the
Hunger Wall (see opposite)
runs southeast from the
funicular to Petřín's **Štefánik
Observatory**. The small
astronomical exhibition inside
is hardly worth bothering
with, but if it's a clear night, a
quick peek through either of
the observatory's two powerful
telescopes is a treat.

ROZHLEDNA

Ⓦ www.petrinska-rozhledna.cz. Daily: April
10am–7pm; May–Sept 10am–10pm; Oct
10am–8pm; Nov–March 10am–6pm. 100Kč.
MAP P.48–49, POCKET MAP B13

Petřín's most familiar landmark
is its look-out tower, or
Rozhledna, an octagonal
interpretation – though a mere
fifth of the size – of the Eiffel
Tower which shocked Paris in
1889, and a tribute to the city's
strong cultural and political
links with Paris at the time. The
view from the public gallery is
terrific in fine weather.

MIRROR MAZE (BLUDIŠTĚ)

Ⓦ www.petrinska-rozhledna.cz. Daily: April
10am–7pm; May–Sept 10am–10pm; Oct
10am–8pm; Nov–March 10am–6pm. 70Kč.
MAP P.48–49, POCKET MAP B13

The **Mirror Maze** is housed
in a mini neo-Gothic
castle complete with mock
drawbridge. As well as a
mirror maze, there is an
action-packed, life-sized
diorama of the victory of
Prague's students and Jews
over the Swedes on the Charles
Bridge in 1648. The humour
of the convex and concave
mirrors that lie beyond the
diorama is so simple it has both
adults and kids giggling away.

(Hladová zeď). Instigated in
the 1460s by Emperor
Charles IV, it was much
lauded at the time as a great
public work which provided
employment for the burgeoning
ranks of the city's destitute
(hence its name); in fact, much
of the wall's construction was
paid for by the expropriation of
Jewish property.

FUNICULAR RAILWAY

MAP P.48–49, POCKET MAP B13–C13

The **funicular railway** (*lanová
dráha*) for Petřín sets off
from a station just off Újezd
and runs every 10–15min
(daily 9am–11.30pm); public
transport tickets and travel
passes are valid. At the
Nebozízek stop halfway up
where the carriages pass each
other you can get out and soak
up the view at the *Nebozízek*
restaurant (see p.58); the top
station is closest to the Mirror
Maze and Rozhledna.

Shops

AHASVER

Prokopská 3. Tues–Sun 11am–6pm.
MAP P.48–49, POCKET MAP D12

A delightful little shop selling antique gowns and jewellery, as well as paintings, porcelain and glass.

ELIMA

Janský vršek 5. Daily 10am–6pm. MAP P.48–49,
POCKET MAP C12

This tiny little shop in the backstreets sells beautiful, inexpensive, hand-made Polish pottery from Boleslawiec (Bunzlau).

FAUX PAS

Újezd 26. Daily 11am–7pm. MAP P.48–49,
POCKET MAP D13

At Faux Pas, designer Jolana Izbická goes in for brightly coloured and provocative clothing, as well as stocking one-off pieces by other central European designers.

GALERIE PIVA

Lázeňská 15. Mon–Sat 11am–7pm.
MAP P.48–49, POCKET MAP D12

This is a relatively small shop, but it stocks one of the city's most judicious selection of Czech bottled beers.

SHAKESPEARE A SYNOVÉ

U lužického semináře 10. Daily 11am–7pm.
MAP P.48–49, POCKET MAP E12

Don't be deceived by the tiny frontage, this is a wonderful, large, rambling well-stocked English-language bookstore in which to while away some time.

TRUHLÁŘ MARIONETY

U lužického semináře 5. Daily 10am–8pm.
MAP P.48–49, POCKET MAP D12

Prague is awash with cheap, and frankly quite gawdy, puppets, but the Truhlář family are a cut above the rest. Wooden marionettes off the peg from 1600Kč – bespoke from 12,000Kč.

VETEŠNICTVÍ

Vítězná 16. Daily 10am–4pm. MAP P.48–49,
POCKET MAP D14

Proper Prague bric-a-brac shop jam-packed with everything from old metal signs and Communist memorabilia to glassware and porcelain.

Cafés

BOHEMIA BAGEL

Lázeňská 19 ⓦ www.bohemiabagel.cz. Daily
7.30am–7pm. MAP P.48–49, POCKET MAP D12

Malá Strana branch of the successful self-service chain (and expat favourite) situated close to Charles Bridge, serving filled bagels, all-day breakfasts, soup and chilli.

CUKRKÁVALIMONÁDA

Lázeňská 7. Daily 8.30am–8pm. MAP P.48–49,
POCKET MAP D12

Very professional and well-run café, serving good brasserie-style dishes, as well as coffee and croissants, with tables overlooking the church of Panna Maria pod řetězem.

CAFÉS ON KAMPA

PEKAŘSTVÍ V KARMELITSKÉ

Karmelitská 20. Mon–Sat 7am–7pm, Sun 10am–6pm. MAP P.48–49. POCKET MAP D12

A classic cheap Czech bakery, just off Malostranské náměstí, with a café attached where you can wash down your cakes, pastries and rolls with a coffee.

SAVOY

Vítězná 5. Mon–Fri 8am–10.30pm, Sat & Sun 9am–10.30pm. MAP P.48–49. POCKET MAP D12

An L-shaped Habsburg-era café from 1893 with a superb, neo-Renaissance ceiling; you can just have a coffee or a snack if you want, but it doubles as a very good restaurant, with mains (including lots of seafood) for 350Kč and above.

U KNOFLÍČKŮ (THE LITTLE BUTTON)

Újezd 17. Mon–Fri 9am–6.30pm, Sat & Sun 10am–6.30pm. MAP P.48–49. POCKET MAP D13

A quaint, slightly chintzy, new *cukrárna* (patisserie) selling ice cream, cakes, coffee and *chlebíčky* (open sandwiches).

U ZELENÉHO ČAJE (THE GREEN TEA)

Nerudova 19. Daily 11am–10pm. MAP P.48–49. POCKET MAP C11

Great little smoke-free stop-off for a pot of tea or a veggie snack en route to Prague Castle; the only problem is getting a place at one of the four tables.

Restaurants

BAR BAR

Všehrdova 17 ☎ 257 312 246. Mon–Thurs & Sun noon–midnight, Fri & Sat noon–2am. MAP P.48–49. POCKET MAP D13

Unpretentious cellar restaurant that specializes in savoury (mostly veggie) pancakes (125–140Kč) and sweet crêpes/ *palačinky* (80Kč). Free wi-fi.

COFFEE AND CAKE AT THE SAVOY CAFÉ

CAFÉ DE PARIS

Maltézské náměstí 4 ☎ 603 160 718. Daily noon–midnight. MAP P.48–49. POCKET MAP D12

This cosy, family-run restaurant is based on the famous *Café de Paris* in Geneva. The menu is very short and the signature dish is beef entrecôte in a creamy sauce composed to a secret recipe (280Kč); there's a tofu version available, too.

DAVID

Tržiště 21 ☎ 257 533 109. Daily 11.30am–11pm. MAP P.48–49. POCKET MAP C12

Tip-top service is guaranteed at this small, formal, family-run restaurant, which specializes in doing classic Bohemian cuisine full justice. The best deal is the three-course fixed menu, which starts at 600Kč.

HERGETOVÁ CIHELNÁ

Cihelná 2b ☎ 296 826 103. Daily 11.30am–1am. MAP P.48–49. POCKET MAP E11

Slick restaurant serving Tiger prawn starters (385Kč), plus tasty pasta and risotto (250–300Kč), and the odd traditional Czech dish (200–400Kč). The riverside summer terrace overlooks Charles Bridge.

KAMPA PARK

Na Kampě 8b ☎ 296 826 102. Daily 11.30am–1am. MAP P.48–49, POCKET MAP E12

Pink house exquisitely located right by the Vltava on Kampa Island, with a superb fish and seafood menu (mains 600–900Kč), top-class service and tables outside in summer.

NEBOZÍZEK (LITTLE AUGER)

Petřínské sady 411 ☎ 257 515 329. Daily 11am–11pm. MAP P.48–49, POCKET MAP C13

Situated at the halfway stop on the Petřín funicular, the view from *Nebozízek* is superb; there's an outdoor terrace and a traditional Czech menu heavy with game dishes from 300Kč.

NOI

Újezd 19 ☎ 257 311 411. Daily 11am–1am. MAP P.48–49, POCKET MAP D13

A stylish, atmospheric restaurant dishing out some of the tastiest, spiciest Thai food in Prague (mains 200–300Kč), though it's not great for vegetarians. There's a lovely courtyard patio round the back.

PÁLFFÝ PALÁC

Valdštejnská 14 ☎ 257 530 522. Daily 11am–11pm. MAP P.48–49, POCKET MAP D11

The restaurant occupies a grand candle-lit room on the first floor of an old Baroque palace, and features a wonderful outdoor terrace from which you can survey the red rooftops of Malá Strana. The international menu is renowned for its venison (main courses 500–700Kč).

RYBÁŘSKÝ KLUB

U Sovových mlýnů 1 ☎ 257 534 200. Daily noon–11pm. MAP P.48–49, POCKET MAP D13

Freshwater fish – carp, catfish, zander and others – baked, grilled or deep fried in breadcrumbs for around 250–400Kč are served up at this unpretentious riverside restaurant situated in the park on Kampa Island.

U MALÉ VELRYBY (THE LITTLE WHALE)

Maltézské náměstí 15 ☎ 257 214 703. Mon–Sat 11am–11pm, Sun 11am–8pm. MAP P.48–49, POCKET MAP D12

Herb-encrusted salmon, succulent steaks and duck (around 300Kč) are all turned out to perfection by the chef at this simple modern restaurant. There's also a tapas menu and freshly bread baked.

U SEDMI ŠVÁBŮ (THE SEVEN SWABIANS)

Janský vršek 14 ☎ 257 531 455. Daily 11am–11pm. MAP P.48–49, POCKET MAP C11

Named after the Grimm brothers' tale, this torch-lit tavern serves up traditional Czech beer and food (150–300Kč) to the occasional accompaniment of medieval shenanigans from fire breathing to sword fighting.

PÁLFFÝ PALÁC

Pubs and bars

BARÁČNICKÁ RYCHTA

Na tržiště 23. Daily noon–midnight.
MAP P.48–49, POCKET MAP C12

Všebaráčnická rychta (as it's also known) is a smoke-free backstreet *pivnice* hidden away in the cobbled streets south of Nerudova – at night, approach from Tržiště.

JO'S BAR

Malostranské náměstí 7. Daily 11am–2am.
MAP P.48–49, POCKET MAP C12

Jo's is the city's original American backpacker hangout. Though it no longer has quite the same vitality, it remains a good place to meet other travellers. There's a club, *Jo's Garáž*, downstairs.

LATIN ART CAFÉ

Janský vršek 2. Daily 2pm–5am. MAP P.48–49,
POCKET MAP C12

A Latino hideout, decked out with Botero prints and tucked away in the backstreets, this café-bar is worth seeking out to hear some great Latin American live music. Free wi-fi.

ST NICHOLAS CAFÉ

Tržiště 10. Mon–Fri 4pm–2am, Sat & Sun 1pm–1am. MAP P.48–49, POCKET MAP C12

A well-dressed older crowd of Czechs and expat diplomatic folk come to this small, vaulted cellar bar for live music, pizza and Pilsner.

TATO KOJKEJ

Kampa Park. Daily 10am–midnight.
MAP P.48–49, POCKET MAP D13

This is a quirky laidback café-bar with mismatched sofas and a nice terrace, in an old mill with its own waterwheel, by the river at the southern end of Kampa's park.

U HROCHA (THE HIPPOPOTAMUS)

Thunovská 10. Daily 11am–11pm. MAP P.48–49,
POCKET MAP C11

A close-knit bunch of locals fill this small, smoky Czech *pivnice* close to the British Embassy, which serves Pilsner Urquell.

U KOCOURA (THE CAT)

Nerudova 2. Daily 11am–11pm. MAP P.48–49,
POCKET MAP D11

The most famous Czech pub on Nerudova inevitably attracts tourists, but the locals come here too for the Pilsner Urquell and Budvar, plus the obvious Czech stomach-fillers.

Venues

MALOSTRANSKÁ BESEDA

Malostranské náměstí 21 ☎ 257 532 092.
Daily 5pm–midnight. MAP P.48–49, POCKET MAP D11

Malá Strana's old town hall has been refurbished and once again be a great venue for Czech rock bands.

U MALÉHO GLENA (LITTLE GLENN'S)

Karmelitská 23 ⓦ www.malyglen.cz. Live music nightly 9.30pm–1am. MAP P.48–49,
POCKET MAP D12

The tiny downstairs stage here hosts an eclectic mix of Latin jazz, bebop and blues. Cover charge 150–200Kč.

U MALÉHO GLENA

Staré Město

Staré Město – literally the "Old Town" – is Prague's most central, vital ingredient. The busiest restaurants and pubs are here, and during the day a gaggle of shoppers and tourists fills its complex and utterly confusing web of narrow byways. Yet despite all the commercial activity, there are still plenty of residential streets, giving the area a lived-in feel that is rarely found in European city centres. At the heart of the district is the Old Town Square (Staroměstské náměstí), Prague's showpiece main square, easily the most magnificent in central Europe, and a great place to get your bearings before heading off into the labyrinthine backstreets. The best approach is from the city's most famous medieval landmark, the statue-encrusted Charles Bridge.

CHARLES BRIDGE (KARLŮV MOST)

MAP P.62–63, POCKET MAP E12

Bristling with statuary and crowded with people, the **Charles Bridge** is by far the city's most famous monument. Built in the fourteenth century by Charles IV, the bridge originally featured just a simple crucifix. The first sculpture wasn't added until 1683, when **St John of Nepomuk** appeared. His statue was such a propaganda success that the Catholic church authorities ordered another 21 to be erected between 1706 and 1714. Individually, only a few of the works are outstanding, but taken collectively, set against the backdrop of the Hrad, the effect is breathtaking.

The bridge is now one of the city's most popular places to hang out, day and night: the crush of sightseers never abates during the day, when the niches

created by the bridge-piers are occupied by souvenir-hawkers and buskers, but at night things calm down a bit, and the views are, if anything, even more spectacular.

You can climb both of the mighty Gothic **bridge towers** for a bird's-eye view of the masses pouring across. The one on the Malá Strana side (April–Sept Mon–Thurs & Sun 10am–6pm, Fri & Sat 10am–7pm; Oct–March daily 10am–6pm; 70Kč) features two unequal towers, connected by a castellated arch, which forms the entrance to the bridge. The Staré Město one (daily: April–Sept 10am–10pm; Nov–March 10am–7pm; 70Kč) is arguably the finer of the two, its eastern facade still encrusted in Gothic cake-like decorations from Peter Parler's workshop.

CHURCH OF SV FRANTIŠEK Z ASSISI (ST FRANCIS OF ASSISI)

Křížovnické náměstí. MAP P.62–63, POCKET MAP F12
Built in the 1680s for the Czech **Order of Knights of the Cross with a Red Star**, the original gatekeepers of the bridge, the interior of this half-brick church is smothered in rich marble and gilded furnishings

and dominated by its huge dome, decorated with a vast fresco of *The Last Judgement* and rich marble furnishings.

CHARLES BRIDGE MUSEUM (MUZEUM KARLOVA MOSTU)

Křížovnické náměstí 3 🚇 www .muzeumkarlovamostu.cz. Daily: April–Sept 10am–8pm; Oct–March 10am–6pm. 150Kč. MAP P.62–63, POCKET MAP F12
Those with an interest in stonemasonry and engineering will enjoy the exhibition; everyone else will probably get more out of the archive film footage.

CHURCH OF SV SALVÁTOR (ST SAVIOUR)

Křížovnické náměstí. MAP P.62–63, POCKET MAP F12
The facade of this church prickles with saintly statues which are lit up enticingly at night. Founded in 1593, it marks the beginning of the Jesuits' rise to power and is part of the Klementinum (see p.64). Like many Jesuit churches, its design copies that of the Gesù church in Rome; it's worth a quick look, if only for the frothy stucco plasterwork and delicate ironwork in its triple-naved interior.

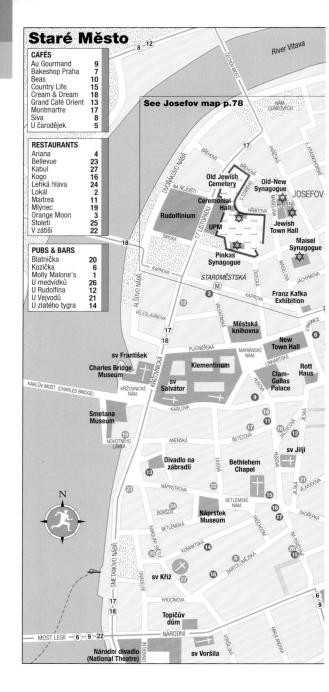

Staré Město

CAFÉS
Au Gourmand	9
Bakeshop Praha	7
Beas	10
Country Life	15
Cream & Dream	18
Grand Café Orient	13
Montmartre	17
Siva	8
U čarodějek	5

RESTAURANTS
Ariana	4
Bellevue	23
Kabul	27
Kogo	16
Lehká hlava	24
Lokál	2
Maitrea	11
Mlýnec	19
Orange Moon	3
Stoleti	25
V zátiší	22

PUBS & BARS
Blatnička	20
Kozička	6
Molly Malone's	1
U medvídků	26
U Rudolfina	12
U Vejvodů	21
U zlatého tygra	14

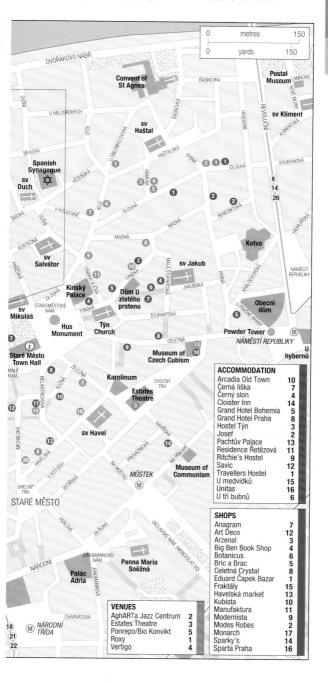

ACCOMMODATION

Arcadia Old Town	10
Černá liška	7
Černý slon	4
Cloister Inn	14
Grand Hotel Bohemia	5
Grand Hotel Praha	8
Hostel Týn	3
Josef	2
Pachtův Palace	13
Residence Řetězová	11
Ritchie's Hostel	9
Savic	12
Travellers Hostel	1
U medvídků	15
Unitas	16
U tří bubnů	6

VENUES

AghARTa Jazz Centrum	2
Estates Theatre	3
Ponrepo/Bio Konvikt	5
Roxy	1
Vertigo	4

SHOPS

Anagram	7
Art Deco	12
Arzenal	3
Big Ben Book Shop	4
Botanicus	6
Bric a Brac	5
Celetná Crystal	8
Eduard Čapek Bazar	1
Fraktály	15
Havelská market	13
Kubista	10
Manufaktura	11
Modernista	9
Modes Robes	2
Monarch	17
Sparky's	14
Sparta Praha	16

KARLOVA

MAP P.62–63, POCKET MAP F12

As the quickest route between the Charles Bridge and the Old Town Square, the narrow street of **Karlova** is packed with people day and night, their attention divided between checking out the tacky souvenir shops and not losing their way. With Europop blaring from several shops, jesters' hats and puppets in abundance, and a strip club for good measure, the whole atmosphere can be a bit oppressive in the height of summer – a more peaceful alternative is to head through the courtyards of the Klementinum.

KLEMENTINUM

Karlova 1 ⓦ www.klementinum.com. Daily 10am–6pm. 220Kč. MAP P.62–63, POCKET MAP F12

As they stroll down Karlova, few people notice the **former Jesuit College** on the north side of the street, which covers an area second in size only to the castle. The Habsburg family summoned the Jesuits to Prague in 1556 to help bolster the Catholic cause in Bohemia, and put them in charge of the entire education system only to expel them in 1773. The complex now belongs to the university and houses, among other things, the **National Library**.

Aside from the ornate **Mirrored Chapel** (Zrcadlová kaple), which is open only for concerts, the Klementinum's most easily accessible attractions are open to the public on a thirty-minute **guided tour** (in English). The most spectacular sight is the **Baroque Library**, a long room lined with leather tomes, whose ceiling is decorated by one continuous illusionistic fresco praising secular wisdom, and whose wrought-iron gallery balustrade is held up by wooden barley-sugar columns. Upstairs, at roughly the centre of the Klementinum complex, is the **Astronomical Tower**, from which you can enjoy a superb view over the centre of Prague.

NEW TOWN HALL (NOVÁ RADNICE)

Mariánské náměstí 2. MAP P.62–63, POCKET MAP F12–G12

The most striking features of the rather severe **New Town Hall** are the two gargantuan Art Nouveau statues which stand guard at either corner. The one on the left, looking like Darth Vader, is the "Iron Knight", mascot of the armourers' guild; to the right is the caricatured sixteenth-century Jewish sage and scholar, **Rabbi Löw**. According to legend, Löw was visited by

Death on several occasions, but escaped his clutches until he reached the ripe old age of 97, when the Grim Reaper hid in a rose innocently given to him by his (in this case, naked) granddaughter. He is also credited with creating the Golem, a mute Frankenstein-type figure, who periodically ran amok in Prague (see p.83).

MALÉ NÁMĚSTÍ

MAP P.62–63, POCKET MAP G12

A little cobbled square at the eastern end of Karlova, **Malé náměstí** was originally settled by French merchants in the twelfth century and is home to the city's first apothecary, **U zlaté koruny** (The Golden Crown), opened by a Florentine in 1353 at no. 13. The former pharmacy boasts chandeliers and a restored Baroque interior, though it's now a jeweller's. The square's best-known building is the russet-red, neo-Renaissance **Rott Haus**, originally an ironmonger's shop founded by V.J. Rott in 1840, whose facade is smothered in agricultural scenes and motifs inspired by the Czech artist Mikuláš Aleš. At the centre of the square stands a (no longer functioning) fountain dating from 1560, which retains its beautiful, original wrought-iron canopy.

CLAM-GALLAS PALACE (CLAM-GALLASŮV PALÁC)

Mariánské náměstí 2 ⓦ www.ahmp.cz. Tues–Sun 10am–6pm. 40Kč. MAP P.62–63, POCKET MAP F12–G12

Despite its size, the **Clam-Gallas Palace** is easy to overlook in a narrow space. It's a typically lavish Baroque affair, with big and burly *Atlantes* supporting the portals. There are regular historical exhibitions, organized by the Prague City Archives, and evening concerts, which allow you to climb the grandiose staircase and have a peek at the sumptuous ceremonial rooms.

STARÉ MĚSTO

STAROMĚSTSKÉ NÁMĚSTÍ (OLD TOWN SQUARE)

MAP P.62–63, POCKET MAP G11–G12

Easily the most spectacular square in Prague, **Staroměstské náměstí** is the traditional heart of the city. Most of the brightly coloured houses look solidly eighteenth century, but their Baroque facades hide considerably older buildings. Over the centuries, the square has seen its fair share of demonstrations and battles: the **27 white crosses** set into the paving commemorate the Protestant leaders who were condemned to death on the orders of the Habsburg Emperor in 1621, while the patch of green grass marks the neo-Gothic east wing of the town hall, burned down by the Nazis on the final day of the Prague Uprising in May 1945. Nowadays, the square is filled with café tables in summer and an ice rink and Christmas market in winter, while tourists pour in all year round to watch the town hall's astronomical clock chime, to sit on the benches in front of the Hus Monument, and to drink in the atmosphere of this historic showpiece.

STARÉ MĚSTO TOWN HALL (STAROMĚSTSKÁ RADNICE)

Staroměstské náměstí 1 MAP P.62–63, POCKET MAP G12

The Staré Město **Town Hall** occupies a whole sequence of houses on Staroměstské náměstí, culminating in an obligatory wedge-tower with a graceful Gothic oriel. It's hardly worth taking the twenty-minute **guided tour** (Mon 11am–6pm, Tues–Sun 9am–6pm; 70Kč) of the few rooms that survived World War II, but it's fun to climb the **tower** (open until 8pm; 100Kč) for the panoramic view across Prague's spires. You can also visit the medieval chapel, which has patches of original wall painting, and wonderful grimacing corbels at the foot of the ribbed vaulting. If you get here just before the clock strikes the hour, you can also watch the Apostles going out on parade.

ASTRONOMICAL CLOCK

Staroměstské náměstí 1. Hourly 9am–9pm. MAP P.62–63, POCKET MAP G12

The most popular feature on Staroměstské náměstí is the town hall's fifteenth-century **Astronomical Clock**, whose hourly mechanical dumbshow regularly attracts a crowd of tourists. Little figures of the Apostles shuffle past the top two windows, bowing to the audience, while perched on pinnacles below are the four threats to the city as perceived by the medieval mind: Death carrying his hourglass and tolling his bell, the Jew with his moneybags (since 1945 shorn of his stereotypical beard and referred to as Greed), Vanity admiring his reflection, and a turbaned Turk shaking his head. Beneath the moving figures, four characters representing Philosophy,

HOUSE FACADE ON STAROMĚSTSKÉ NÁMĚSTÍ

Religion, Astronomy and History stand motionless throughout the performance. Finally, a cockerel pops out and flaps its wings to signal that the show's over; the clock then chimes the hour.

HUS MONUMENT

Staroměstské náměstí. MAP P.62–63. POCKET MAP G12

The colossal **Jan Hus Monument** features a turbulent sea of blackened bodies – the oppressed to his right, the defiant to his left – out of which rises the majestic moral authority of Hus himself, a radical religious reformer and martyr from the fifteenth century. On the 500th anniversary of his death in 1915, the statue was unveiled, but the Austrians refused to hold an official ceremony; in protest, Praguers smothered the monument in flowers. Since then it has been a powerful symbol of Czech nationalism: in March 1939, it was draped in swastikas by the invading Nazis, and in August 1968, it was shrouded in funereal black by Praguers, protesting at the Soviet invasion. The inscription along the base is a quote from the will of Comenius (see p.50), one of Hus's seventeenth-century followers, and includes Hus's most famous dictum, *Pravda vitězí* (Truth Prevails), which has been the motto of just about every Czech revolution since then.

CHURCH OF SV MIKULÁŠ

Staroměstské náměstí. Daily 10am–4pm. MAP P.62–63, POCKET MAP G11–12

The destruction of the east wing of the town hall in 1945 rudely exposed the Baroque church of **sv Mikuláš**, built for the Benedictines in 1735. The south front is decidedly luscious, with blackened statuary at every cornice; inside, however, it's a much smaller space, theatrically organized into a series of interlocking curves. It's also rather plainly furnished, partly because it was closed down by Joseph II and turned into a storehouse, and partly because it's now owned by the very "low", modern, Czechoslovak Hussite Church. Instead, your eyes are drawn sharply upwards to the impressive stuccowork, the wrought-iron galleries and the trompe-l'oeil frescoes on the dome.

KINSKÝ PALACE

Staroměstské náměstí 12 ⓦ www.ngprague .cz. Tues–Sun 10am–6pm. 150Kč. MAP P.62–63, POCKET MAP G11

The largest secular building on Staroměstské náměstí is the Rococo **Kinský Palace**, which is perhaps most notorious as the venue for the fateful speech by the Communist prime minister, **Klement Gottwald**, who walked out onto the grey stone balcony one snowy February morning in 1948, flanked by his Party henchmen, to celebrate the Communist takeover with the thousands of enthusiastic supporters who packed the square below. The top two floors currently house a vast permanent collection of Asian art.

TÝN CHURCH (TÝNSKÝ CHRÁM)

Celetná 5 ⓦ tynska.farnost.cz. Daily 10am–1pm & 3–5pm. Free. MAP P.62, POCKET MAP G12

The mighty **Týn church** is by far the most imposing Gothic structure in the Staré Město. Its two irregular towers, bristling with baubles, spires and pinnacles, rise like giant antennae above the arcaded houses which otherwise obscure its facade, and are spectacularly lit up at night. Inside, the church has a lofty, narrow nave punctuated at ground level by black and gold Baroque altarpieces. One or two original Gothic furnishings survive, most notably the pulpit and the fifteenth-century baldachin, housing a winged altar in the north aisle. Behind the pulpit, you'll find another superb winged altar depicting John the Baptist, dating from 1520. The pillar on the right of the chancel steps contains the red marble tomb of **Tycho Brahe**, court astronomer to Rudolf II.

TÝN COURTYARD

MAP P.62–63, POCKET MAP G11

Hidden behind the Týn church is the **Týn courtyard**, also known by its German name, **Ungelt** (meaning "No Money", a pseudonym used to deter marauding invaders), which, as the trading base of German merchants, was one of the first settlements on the Vltava. Later, it was transformed into a palace, only to fall into disrepair under the Communists. The complex has now come full circle and is once again home to various shops, restaurants, hotels and the Dominicans.

CHURCH OF SV JAKUB

Malá Štupartská 6. Daily 9.30am–noon & 2–4pm. Free. MAP P.62–63, POCKET MAP H11

Before entering the church make sure you admire the distinctive bubbling, stucco portal above the main entrance. The church's massive Gothic proportions – it has the longest nave in Prague after the cathedral – make it a favourite venue for organ recitals and other concerts. After the great

CHURCH OF SV JAKUB

fire of 1689, Prague's Baroque artists remodelled the entire interior, adding huge pilasters, a series of colourful frescoes and over twenty side altars. The church has close historical links with the butchers of Prague, who are responsible for the thoroughly decomposed human forearm hanging high up on the west wall, on the right as you enter. It has been here for over four hundred years now, ever since a thief tried to steal the jewels of the Madonna from the high altar. As the thief reached out, the Virgin supposedly grabbed his arm and refused to let go. The next day the congregation of butchers had no option but to lop it off, and it has hung there as a warning ever since.

CONVENT OF ST AGNES (ANEŽSKÝ KLÁŠTER)

Anežská 12 ⓦ www.ngprague.cz. Tues–Sun 10am–6pm. 150Kč. MAP P.62–63, POCKET MAP H10
Prague's oldest surviving Gothic building, founded in 1233 as a Franciscan convent for the Order of the Poor Clares, now provides a fittingly atmospheric setting

for the city's chief **medieval art collection**. The exhibition is arranged chronologically, starting with a remarkable silver-gilt casket from 1360 used to house the skull of St Ludmila. The nine panels from the Vyšší Brod altarpiece, from around 1350, are also among the finest in central Europe. The real gems of the collection, however, are the six panels by Master Theodoric, who painted over one hundred such paintings for Charles IV's castle chapel at Karlštejn. These larger-than-life, half-length portraits of saints, church fathers and so on are full of intense expression and richly coloured detail, their depictions spilling onto the embossed frames. For a glimpse of some extraordinary draughtsmanship, check out the woodcuts by the likes of Cranach the Elder and Dürer – the seven-headed beast in Dürer's *Apocalypse* cycle is particularly Harry Potter. As you exit, you get to see the inside of the Gothic cloisters and the bare church that serves as a resting place for, among others, Václav I (1205–53) and St Agnes herself.

MUSEUM OF CZECH CUBISM
(MUZEUM ČESKÉHO KUBISMU)

Ovocný trh 19 ⓦ www.ngprague.cz. Tues–Sun 10am–6pm. 100Kč. MAP P.62–63, POCKET MAP H12

The museum is housed in **Dům U černé Matky boží** (House at the Black Madonna), built as a department store in 1911–12 by Josef Gočár and one of the best examples of Czech Cubist architecture in Prague. The permanent collection on the top two floors has a little bit of everything that the short-lived Czech Cubist movement produced, from sofas and sideboards by Gočár himself to paintings by Emil Filla and Josef Čapek, plus some wonderful sculptures by Otto Gutfreund and models of the Cubist villas in Vyšehrad (see p.108).

ESTATES THEATRE
(STAVOVSKÉ DIVADLO)

Ovocný trh 1. MAP P.62–63, POCKET MAP H12

The lime-green and white **Estates Theatre** was built in the early 1780s for the entertainment of Prague's large and powerful German community and remains one of the finest Neoclassical buildings in Prague, reflecting the enormous self-confidence of its patrons. The theatre has a place in Czech history, too, however, for it was here that the **Czech national anthem**, "Kde domov můj?" ("Where is my Home?"), was first performed. It is also a place of pilgrimage for Mozart fans, since it was here that the premieres of *Don Giovanni* and *La Clemenza di Tito* took place – the statue of a hooded figure by the entrance commemorates the fact. This is, in fact, one of the few opera houses in Europe that remains intact from Mozart's time (though it underwent major refurbishment during the nineteenth century), and it was used by Miloš Forman to film the concert scenes for his Oscar-laden *Amadeus*.

BETHLEHEM CHAPEL
(BETLÉMSKÁ KAPLE)

Betlémské náměstí 4. Tues–Sun: April–Oct 10am–6.30pm; Nov–March 10am–5.30pm. 50Kč. MAP P.62–63, POCKET MAP F13

The **Bethlehem Chapel** was founded in 1391 by religious reformists, who, denied the right to build a church, proceeded instead to build the largest chapel in Bohemia, with a total capacity of exactly 3000. Sermons were delivered not in the customary Latin, but in the language of the masses – Czech. From 1402 to 1413, **Jan Hus** preached here, regularly pulling in more than enough commoners to fill the chapel, while the Anabaptist **Thomas Müntzer** also preached here in 1521. Of the original building, only the three outer walls remain, with restored patches of the biblical scenes which were used to get the message across to the illiterate congregation. The rest is a scrupulous reconstruction, using the original plans and a fair amount of imaginative guesswork.

NÁPRSTEK MUSEUM

Betlémské náměstí 1 ⓦ www.aconet.cz /npm. Tues–Sun 10am–6pm. 80Kč. MAP P.62–63, POCKET MAP H13

Vojta Náprstek, founder of the Náprstek Museum, was inspired by the great Victorian museums of London and turned the family brewery into a museum, initially intending it to concentrate on the virtues of industrial progress. Náprstek's interests gradually shifted towards anthropology, however, and it is his ethnographic collections from the Americas, Australasia and Oceania that are now displayed in the museum. Despite the fact that the museum could clearly do with an injection of cash, it still manages to put on some really excellent temporary ethnographic exhibitions on the ground floor, and also does a useful job of promoting tolerance of different cultures.

SMETANA MUSEUM (MUZEUM BEDŘICHA SMETANY)

Novotného lávka 1 ⓦ www.nm.cz. Daily except Tues 10am–noon & 12.30–5pm. 50Kč. MAP P.62–63, POCKET MAP F12

Housed in a gaily decorated neo-Renaissance building on the riverfront, the **Smetana Museum** celebrates the life and work of the most nationalist of all the great Czech composers. He enjoyed his greatest success as a composer with *The Bartered Bride*, which marked the birth of Czech opera, but he was forced to give up conducting in 1874 with the onset of deafness, and eventually died of syphilis in a mental asylum. Unfortunately, the museum fails to capture much of the spirit of the man, though the views across to the castle are good, and you get to wave a laser baton around in order to listen to his music.

THE ESTATES THEATRE

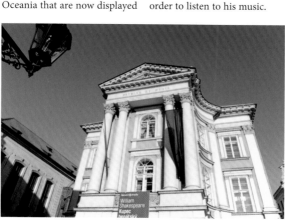

Shops

ANAGRAM

Týn 4. Mon–Sat 10am–8pm, Sun 10am–7pm.
MAP P.62–63, POCKET MAP H11

Friendly English-language bookstore which has lots of Czech authors in translation and books on Czech politics and culture, plus a small secondhand section.

ART DECO

Michalská 21. Mon–Fri 2–7pm. MAP P.62–63,
POCKET MAP G12

A stylish antique shop crammed with a wonderful mixture of clothes, hats, mufflers, teapots, glasses, clocks and art from the first half of the twentieth century.

ARZENAL

Valentinská 11. Daily 10am–midnight.
MAP P.62–63 POCKET MAP F11.

Lots of fancy furniture, kitchenware and glassware by leading Czech designer, Bořek Šípek, inside a Thai/Japanese restaurant.

ART DECO SHOP

BIG BEN BOOK SHOP

Malá Štupartská 5. Mon–Fri 9am–8pm,
Sat 10am–8pm, Sun 11am–6pm. MAP P.62–63
POCKET MAP H11.

Bookstore with probably the widest selection in the city, including cheap paperbacks, kids' books, and lots of magazines and papers.

BOTANICUS

Týn 3. Daily 10am–6.30pm. MAP P.62–63.
POCKET MAP H11

Czech take on the UK's Body Shop, with a more folksy ambience. Dried flowers, handmade paper and fancy honey are sold alongside natural soaps and shampoos.

BRIC A BRAC

Týnská 7. Daily 10am–6pm. MAP P.62–63.
POCKET MAP G11

Absolutely minute antique store, packed to the very rafters with every conceivable trinket. The central location means that prices are quite high, but the place is worth visiting for the spectacle alone. The owner also runs a larger place round the corner.

CELETNÁ CRYSTAL

Celetná 15. Daily 10am–7pm. MAP P.62–63.
POCKET MAP H12

If you're genuinely interested in buying some of the ubiquitous crystal or porcelain that clogs up the city's shop windows, you're sure to get top-quality goods here.

EDUARD ČAPEK BAZAR

Dlouhá 32. Daily noon–10pm. MAP P.62–63.
POCKET MAP H11

Opened in 1911 (and privately owned even under the Communists), this place is a relic in itself, selling quality junk from old domestic utensils and battered tea cups to tools and lamps.

FRAKTÁLY

Betlémské náměstí 5. Mon–Sat 10am–8pm, Sun noon–8pm. MAP P.62–63, POCKET MAP F13

Great bookshop with stylish armchairs to collapse into and peruse books on design, architecture and fine art, or a good place to pick up a poster or arty gift.

HAVELSKÁ MARKET

Havelská. Mon–Fri 8am–6pm, Sat & Sun 9am–6pm. MAP P.62–63, POCKET MAP G12

Open-air market that stretches the full length of the arcaded street of Havelská, selling fruit, flowers, vegetables, CDs, souvenirs and wooden toys.

KUBISTA

Ovocný trh 19. Tues–Sun 10am–6.30pm. MAP P.62–63, POCKET MAP H12

Beautiful shop housed in the same building as the Museum of Czech Cubism and selling reproductions of some of its exquisite Cubist ceramics, jewellery and furniture.

MANUFAKTURA

Melantrichova 17. Daily 10am–8pm. MAP P.62–63, POCKET MAP G12

Czech folk-inspired shop with a fantastic array of traditional wooden toys, painted Easter eggs, straw decorations, honeycomb candles and sundry kitchen utensils.

MODERNISTA

Celetná 12. Daily 11am–7pm. MAP P.62–63, POCKET MAP H12

Beautiful but pricey emporium selling top-drawer restored Czech furniture and furnishings in the functionalist and Cubist styles popular between the wars and beyond.

MODES ROBES

Benediktská 5. Mon–Fri 10am–7pm, Sat 10am–4pm. MAP P.62–63, POCKET MAP H11

Women's boutique whose

SPARTA PRAHA SHOP

interior is smothered in crazy, arty murals – best of all, you can have a coffee while trying on the clothes.

MONARCH

Na Perštýně 15. Mon–Sat noon–8pm. MAP P.62–63, POCKET MAP G13

The city's number one wine shop (and wine bar), with stock from all over the world as well as local wine – it sells cheese and dried meats, too.

SPARKY'S

Havířská 2. Mon–Sat 10am–7pm, Sun 10am–6pm. MAP P.62–63, POCKET MAP H12

Prague's top *dům hraček* (House of Toys) on four floors, which stocks everything from the latest high-tech playthings to traditional wooden toys.

SPARTA PRAHA

Betlémské náměstí 7. Mon–Thurs 10am–5pm, Fri 10am–4pm. MAP P.62–63, POCKET MAP G13

Centrally located football fan shop stocking everything from soccer shirts to ashtrays, mostly for Sparta Praha, but also stocks Slavia Praha, Bohemians and Dukla Praha merchandise.

Cafés

AU GOURMAND

Dlouhá 10 & Rytířská 22. Mon–Fri 8am–7pm,
Sat 8.30am–7pm, Sun 9am–7pm. MAP P.62–63,
POCKET MAP G11

Beautifully tiled French
boulangerie, patisserie and
traiteur selling wickedly
delicious pastries; take-away
or eat-in. Branches in Pasáž
Myslbek at Na příkopě 19 and
in Palladium.

BAKESHOP PRAHA

Kozí 1. Daily 7am–7pm. MAP P.62–63,
POCKET MAP G11

Top-class expat bakery serving
excellent bread, sandwiches
and wraps (100–200Kč), as
well as tarts and cakes, which
you can either take away or
wash down with coffee whilst
reading the papers.

BAKESHOP PRAHA

BEAS

Týnská 19. Mon–Fri 11am–8pm, Sat noon–8pm,
Sun noon–6pm. MAP P.62–63, POCKET MAP H11

Bright, modern Indian veggie
café through the courtyard
off Týnská, offering authentic
dosas and thalis served on
traditional metal trays.

COUNTRY LIFE

Melantrichova 15. Mon–Thurs 10.30am–8pm,
Fri 9am–3pm, Sun noon–6pm. MAP P.62–63,
POCKET MAP G12

Self-service café behind the
health-food shop of the same
name: pile up your plate with
hot or cold dishes and salad
and pay by weight.

CREAM AND DREAM

Husova 12. Daily 11am–10pm. MAP P.62–63,
POCKET MAP G12

Multinational *gelateria* chain
that serves up some of the best
ice cream in Prague, with real
fruit and no artificial rubbish.

GRAND CAFÉ ORIENT

Ovocný trh 19. Mon–Fri 9am–10pm, Sat &
Sun 10am–10pm. MAP P.62–63, POCKET MAP H12

This superb reconstruction
of a famous Cubist café from
1911, on the first floor of the
Museum of Czech Cubism,
dishes up cakes, pancakes and
coffee.

MONTMARTRE

Řetězová 7. Mon–Fri 9am–11pm, Sat & Sun
noon–11pm. MAP P.62–63, POCKET MAP F12

Classic, small, barrel-vaulted
café, the "Montík" was once a
famous First Republic dance
and cabaret venue, frequented
by the likes of Werfel, Jesenská
and Hašek. Nowadays, it's a
lot quieter, attracting a good
mix of students and older
bohos lounging on its adhoc
furniture.

SIVA

Masná 8. Mon–Fri noon–11.30pm, Sat
2–11.30pm, Sun 2–10pm. MAP P.62–63,
POCKET MAP H11

A fair stab at a teahouse
cellar-den complete with
hookah pipes, scatter cushions
and passable Arab snacks.

U ČARODĚJEK

Rámová 4. Daily 11am–11pm. MAP P.62–63,
POCKET MAP H11

Cosy, vaulted, self-styled
literární kavárna, which serves
simple snack dishes for around
100kč, and is popular at lunch
with local office workers.

Restaurants

ARIANA

Rámová 6 ☎ 222 323 438. Daily 11am–11pm.
MAP P.62–63, POCKET MAP H11

Welcoming Afghan restaurant serving up authentic spicy kebabs and veggie dishes (180–250Kč) a stone's throw from the Old Town Square.

BELLEVUE

Smetanovo nábřeží 18 ☎ 222 221 443.
Daily noon–3pm & 5.30–11pm. MAP P.62–63,
POCKET MAP F13

The view of Charles Bridge and the Hrad is outstanding, the setting is very formal and the international cuisine is imaginatively prepared – main courses are 500–700Kč and you need to book ahead.

KABUL

Karoliny Světlé 14 ☎ 224 235 452. Daily noon–11pm. MAP P.62–63, POCKET MAP F13

Small Afghan café-restaurant that serves up homely, simple grilled meats, aubergine and okra dishes (150–300Kč), with hot poppy-seed covered flat bread.

KOGO

Havelská 27 ☎ 224 214 543, ⓦ www.kogo.cz.
Mon–Fri 8am–11pm, Sat & Sun 9am–11pm.
MAP P.62–63, POCKET MAP G12

Divided into two intimate spaces by a passageway, and with a small courtyard out back, this place offers decent pasta, pizza and salads for around 250Kč, served by courteous and efficient waiters.

LEHKÁ HLAVA (CLEAR HEAD)

Boršov 2 ☎ 222 220 665, ⓦ www.lehkahlava
.cz. Mon–Fri 11.30am–11.30pm, Sat & Sun
noon–11.30pm. MAP P.62–63, POCKET MAP F13

Exotic cave-like vegetarian restaurant, just off Karoliny Světlé, offering tapas, soups,

KOGO RESTAURANT

salads and Mediterranean dishes for 125–175Kč.

LOKÁL

Dlouhá 33 ☎ 222 316 265. Mon–Fri
11am–1am, Sat noon–1am, Sun noon–10pm.
MAP P.62–63, POCKET MAP H11

Vast corridor of a restaurant, decked out in sleek, minimalist decor, with waiters in formal long white aprons. What it's actually trying to be is a traditional local pub (no smoking at lunchtimes), serving up excellent Czech pub food for around 100Kč, plus unpasteurized Pilsner Urquell. Free wi-fi.

LEHKÁ HLAVA RESTAURANT

MAITREA

Týnská ulička 6 ☎ 221 711 631. Mon–Fri 11.30am–11.30pm, Sat & Sun noon–11.30pm. MAP P.62–63, POCKET MAP G11

Larger, more luxurious branch of *Lehká hlava*, a den of stylish Buddhist calm serving global vegetarian dishes (125–150Kč).

MLÝNEC

Novotného lávka 9 ☎ 277 000 777. Daily noon–3pm & 5.30–11pm. MAP P.62–63, POCKET MAP F12

A pricey place (which has occasionally garnered Michelin stars) with a fabulous riverside terrace overlooking the Charles Bridge and the Hrad. Czech staples like crispy duck are interspersed with Asian fusion dishes. Mains 500–700Kč.

ORANGE MOON

Rámová 5 ☎ 222 325 119. Daily 11.30am–11.30pm. MAP P.62–63, POCKET MAP H11

Popular, unpretentious Burmese restaurant serving spicy curries from all over the subcontinent for around 200Kč, washed down with Czech beer.

STOLETI

Karoliny Světlé 21 ☎ 222 220 008. ⓦ www .stoleti.cz. Daily noon–midnight. MAP P.62–63, POCKET MAP F13

Imaginative Czech cuisine named after stars of film and stage served in an unstuffy, simply furnished restaurant. Mains around 200Kč.

V ZÁTIŠÍ (STILL LIFE)

Liliová 1 ☎ 222 221 155. Daily noon–3pm & 5.30–11pm. MAP P.62–63, POCKET MAP F13.

Intimate but elegant living-room-sized restaurant serving exquisitely prepared international cuisine, all served in tasty morsels for around 900Kč for two courses.

Pubs and bars

BLATNIČKA

Michalská 5. Daily 11am–11pm. MAP P.62–63, POCKET MAP G12

Long-established wine shop where you can drink straight from the barrel, take away, or head next door to the popular basement *vinárna* for more wine and inexpensive snacks.

KOZIČKA

KOZIČKA

Kozí 4. Mon–Fri noon–4am, Sat 6pm–4am, Sun 7pm–3am. MAP P.62–63, POCKET MAP G11

Busy, designer bare-brick cellar bar with cheap Czech food, tucked away just a short walk from Staroměstské náměstí.

MOLLY MALONE'S

U Obecního dvora 4. Mon–Thurs & Sun 11am–1am, Fri & Sat 11am–2am. MAP P.62–63, POCKET MAP G11

The best of Prague's Irish pubs, with real Irish staff, an open fire, draught Kilkenny and Guinness, and decent Irish-themed food. Free wi-fi.

U MEDVÍDKŮ (THE LITTLE BEARS)

Na Perštýně 7. Mon–Fri 11am–11pm, Sat 11.30am–11pm, Sun 11.30am–10pm. MAP P.62–63, POCKET MAP G13

A Prague beer hall going back to the thirteenth century and still much the same as it always was (make sure you turn right when you enter, and avoid the bar to the left). The Budvar comes thick and fast, and the food is reliably Bohemian.

U RUDOLFINA

Křížovnická 10. Daily 11am–11pm. MAP P.62–63, POCKET MAP F11

A proper Czech *pivnice* serving beautifully-kept Pilsner Urquell and typical pub grub, very close to the Charles Bridge.

U VEJVODŮ

Jilská 4 ☻ www.restauraceuvejvodu.cz. Mon–Thurs 10am–3am, Fri & Sat 10am–4am, Sun 10am–2am. MAP P.62–63, POCKET MAP G13

This atmospheric vaulted beer hall is one of Pilsner Urquell's very successful chain of pubs, serving upmarket pub food.

U ZLATÉHO TYGRA (THE GOLDEN TIGER)

Husova 17. Daily 3pm–midnight. MAP P.62–63, POCKET MAP F12

Small central *pivnice* always busy with locals and tourists trying to get a seat; the late writer and bohemian, Bohumil Hrabal, was a semi-permanent resident.

Clubs and venues

AGHARTA JAZZ CENTRUM

Železná 16 ☎ 222 211 275, ☻ www.agharta .cz. Daily 7pm–1am. MAP P.62–63, POCKET MAP G12

Probably the best jazz club in Prague, with a good mix of Czechs and foreigners and a consistently good programme of gigs, plus a round-the-year festival that brings in some top acts. Cover charge 250Kč.

ESTATES THEATRE (STAVOVSKÉ DIVADLO)

Ovocný trh 1 ☎ 224 901 448, ☻ www .narodni-divadlo.cz. MAP P.62–63, POCKET MAP H12

Prague's oldest opera house has

a glorious nineteenth-century interior and puts on a mixture of theatre, ballet and opera (with English surtitles).

PONREPO/BIO KONVIKT

Bartolomějská 11 ☎ 226 211 866, ☻ www .bio-ponrepo.cz. MAP P.62–63, POCKET MAP F12

Really old classics from the black-and-white era, dug out from the National Film Archives. You need to be a member to visit; membership cards (150Kč) can only be bought Mon–Fri 3–6pm (bring a passport photo).

ROXY

Dlouhá 33 ☎ 224 826 296, ☻ www.roxy.cz. Daily from 7pm. MAP P.62–63, POCKET MAP H11

The centrally located *Roxy* is a great little venue: a laidback, rambling old theatre with an interesting programme of events from arty films and exhibitions to exceptional live acts and top DJ nights. Cover varies: free–250Kč.

ROXY THEATRE

VERTIGO

Havelská 4 ☎ 744 744 255, ☻ www .vertigo-club.cz. Daily 9pm–4am. MAP P.62–63, POCKET MAP G12

Very central club with a decent dance floor and sound system, and an eclectic rota of themed nights.

Josefov

The old Jewish ghetto district of Josefov remains one of the most remarkable sights in Prague and an essential slice of the city's cultural heritage. Although the warren-like street plan of the old ghetto was demolished in the 1890s to make way for streets of luxurious five-storey mansions, six synagogues, the Jewish town hall and the medieval cemetery still survive. They were preserved under the Nazis as a record of communities they had destroyed. To this end, Jewish artefacts from Czechoslovakia and beyond were gathered here, and today make up one of the most comprehensive collections of Judaica in Europe.

FRANZ KAFKA EXHIBITION (EXPOZICE FRANZE KAFKY)

U radnice 5. Tues–Fri 10am–6pm, Sat 10am–5pm. 50Kč. MAP BELOW, POCKET MAP G11

The Czech–German writer Franz Kafka was born on July 3, 1883, above the *Batalion*

Schnapps bar on the corner of Maiselova and Kaprova. The original building has long since been torn down, but a gaunt-looking modern bust now commemorates the site, next to which is the **Frank**

OLD-NEW SYNAGOGUE (STARONOVÁ SYNAGOGA)

Červená 2. Daily except Sat: April–Oct 9am–6pm; Nov–March 9am–4.30pm. 200Kč.
MAP OPPOSITE, POCKET MAP G11

The **Old-New Synagogue** (**Staronová synagoga** or Altneuschul) got its strange name from the fact that when it was built it was indeed very new, though eventually it became the oldest synagogue in Josefov. Begun in the second half of the thirteenth century, and featuring a wonderful set of steep, sawtooth brick gables, it is, in fact, the oldest functioning synagogue in Europe, one of the earliest Gothic buildings in Prague and still the religious centre for Prague's Orthodox Jews. To get to the **main hall**, you must pass through one of the two low vestibules from which women watch the proceedings through narrow slits. Above the entrance is an elaborate tympanum covered in the twisting branches of a vine tree, its twelve bunches of grapes representing the tribes of Israel. The simple, plain interior is mostly taken up with the elaborate wrought-iron cage enclosing the bimah in the centre. The tattered red standard on display was originally a gift to the community from Emperor Ferdinand II for helping fend off the Swedes in 1648.

Kafka Exhibition, a modest exhibition retelling Kafka's life simply but effectively with pictures and quotes. Kafka spent most of his life living in and around Josefov, studying at a German Gymnasium on Old Town Square and working as an accident insurance clerk, until he was forced to retire through ill health in 1922. He died of tuberculosis at the age of 40 in a sanatorium just outside Vienna two years later, and is buried in the New Jewish Cemetery in Žižkov (see p.114). If you've an interest in Kafka, the larger, more sophisticated Kafka museum over in Malá Strana is worth visiting (see p.51).

Visiting Josefov's sights

All the major sights of Josefov – the Old-New Synagogue, Old Jewish Cemetery, the Ceremonial Hall, the Maisel, Pinkas, Klausen and Spanish synagogues – are part of the **Jewish Museum** (ⓦwww .jewishmuseum.cz) and covered by an **all-in-one ticket**, available from any of the quarter's numerous **ticket offices**. This costs 480Kč including the Old-New Synagogue, or 300Kč without. **Opening hours** vary but are basically daily except Saturday April–October 9am–6pm and November–March 9am–4.30pm.

JEWISH TOWN HALL (ŽIDOVSKÁ RADNICE)

Maiselova 18. Not open to the public. MAP P.78, POCKET MAP G11

The **Jewish Town Hall** is one of the few such buildings in central Europe to survive the Holocaust. Founded and funded by Mordecai Maisel, minister of finance to Rudolf II, in the sixteenth century, it was later rebuilt as the creamy-pink Baroque house you now see. The belfry has a clock on each of its four sides, plus a Hebrew one, stuck on the north gable, which, like the Hebrew script, goes "backwards".

MAISEL SYNAGOGUE (MAISELOVA SYNAGOGA)

Maiselova 10. MAP P.78, POCKET MAP G11

Like the town hall, the neo-Gothic **Maisel Synagogue** was founded and paid for entirely by Mordecai Maisel. Set back from the neighbouring houses south down Maiselova, the synagogue was, in its day, one of the most ornate in Josefov. Nowadays, its bare whitewashed neo-Gothic interior houses an exhibition on the history of the Czech–Jewish community up until the 1781 Edict of Tolerance. Along with glass cabinets filled with gold and silverwork, Hanukkah candlesticks, Torah scrolls and other religious artefacts, there's also an example of the antiquated ruffs that had to be worn by all unmarried males from the age of twelve, and a copy of Ferdinand I's decree enforcing the wearing of a circular yellow badge.

PINKAS SYNAGOGUE (PINKASOV SYNAGOGA)

Široká 3. MAP P.78, POCKET MAP F11

Built in the 1530s for the powerful Horovitz family, the **Pinkas Synagogue** has undergone countless restorations over the centuries. In 1958, the synagogue was transformed into a chilling memorial to the 77,297 Czech Jews killed during the Holocaust. The memorial was closed shortly after the 1967 Six Day War – due to damp, according to the Communists – and remained so, allegedly due to problems with the masonry, until it was finally, painstakingly restored in the 1990s. All that remains of the synagogue's original decor today is the ornate bimah surrounded by a beautiful wrought-iron grille, supported by barley-sugar columns.

Of all the sights of the Jewish quarter, the **Holocaust memorial** is perhaps the most moving, with every bit of wall space taken up with the carved stone list of victims, stating simply their name, date of birth and date of death or transportation to the camps. It is the longest epitaph in the world, yet it represents a mere fraction of those who died in the Nazi concentration camps. Upstairs in a room beside the women's gallery, there's also a harrowing exhibition of drawings by children from the Jewish ghetto in Terezín, most of whom were killed in the camps.

OLD JEWISH CEMETERY (STARÝ ŽIDOVSKÝ HŘBITOV)

Široká 3. MAP P.78, POCKET MAP F11

At the heart of Josefov is the **Old Jewish Cemetery**, which you enter from the Pinkas Synagogue and leave by the Klausen Synagogue. Established in the fifteenth century, it was in use until 1787, by which time there were an estimated 100,000 people buried here, one on top of the other, six palms apart, and as many as twelve layers deep. The enormous number of visitors has meant that the graves themselves have been roped off to

protect them, but if you get there before the crowds – a difficult task for much of the year – the cemetery can be a poignant reminder of the ghetto, its inhabitants subjected to inhuman overcrowding even in death. The rest of Prague recedes beyond the tall ash trees and cramped perimeter walls, the haphazard headstones and Hebrew inscriptions casting a powerful spell. On many graves you'll see pebbles, some holding down *kvitlech* or small messages of supplication.

CEREMONIAL HALL (OBŘADNÍ SÍN)

U starého hřbitova. MAP P.78, POCKET MAP F11

Immediately on your left as you leave the cemetery is the **Ceremonial Hall**, a lugubrious neo-Renaissance house built in 1906 as a ceremonial hall by the Jewish Burial Society. Appropriately enough, it's now devoted to an exhibition on Jewish traditions of burial and death, though it would probably be more useful if you could visit it before heading into the cemetery, rather than after.

KLAUSEN SYNAGOGUE (KLAUSOVA SYNAGOGA)

U starého hřbitova 1. MAP P.78, POCKET MAP F11

A late seventeenth-century building, the **Klausen Synagogue** was founded in the 1690s by Mordecai Maisel on the site of several small buildings (Klausen), in what was then a notorious red-light district of Josefov. The ornate Baroque interior contains a rich display of religious objects from embroidered *kippah* to Kiddush cups, and explains the very basics of Jewish religious practice, and the chief festivals or High Holidays.

PAŘÍŽSKA

PAŘÍŽSKA

MAP P.78, POCKET MAP F10–G11

Running through the heart of the old ghetto is **Pařížská**, the ultimate bourgeois avenue, lined with buildings covered in a riot of late nineteenth-century sculpturing, spikes and turrets. At odds with the rest of Josefov, its ground-floor premises are home to designer label clothes and accessory shops, jewellery stores and swanky cafés, restaurants and bars.

SPANISH SYNAGOGUE (ŠPANĚLSKÁ SYNAGOGA)

Vězeňská 1. MAP P.78, POCKET MAP G11

Begun in 1868, the **Spanish Synagogue** is by far the most ornate synagogue in Josefov, its stunning, gilded Moorish interior deliberately imitating the Alhambra (hence its name). Every available surface is smothered with a profusion of floral motifs and geometric patterns, in vibrant reds, greens and blues, which are repeated in the synagogue's huge stained-glass windows. The synagogue now houses an interesting exhibition on the history of Prague's Jews from the time of the 1781 Edict of Tolerance to the Holocaust.

Lovely, slender, painted cast-iron columns hold up the women's gallery, where the displays include a fascinating set of photos depicting the old ghetto at the time of its demolition. There's a section on Prague's German–Jewish writers, including Kafka, and information on the Holocaust. In the upper floor prayer hall, on the first floor, there's an exhibition of silver religious artefacts, a fraction of the six thousand pieces collected here, initially for Prague's Jewish Museum, founded in 1906, and later under the Nazis.

RUDOLFINUM

Alšovo nábřeží 12. Tues–Sun 10am–6pm. MAP P.78, POCKET MAP F11

The **Rudolfinum**, or House of Artists (Dům umělců), is one of the proud civic buildings of the nineteenth-century Czech national revival. Built to house an art gallery, museum and concert hall for the Czech-speaking community, it became the seat of the new Czechoslovak parliament from 1919 until 1941 when it was closed down by the Nazis. Since 1946, the building has returned to its original artistic purpose and it's now one of the capital's main concert venues (home to the Czech Philharmonic) and exhibition spaces.

UPM (MUSEUM OF DECORATIVE ARTS)

17 listopadu 2 ⓦ www.upm.cz. Tues 10am–7pm, Wed–Sun 10am–6pm. 120Kč. MAP P.78, POCKET MAP F11

From its foundation in 1885 through to the end of the First Republic, the **Uměleckoprůmyslové muzeum** or **UPM** received the best that the Czech modern movement had to offer – from Art Nouveau

of Emperor Franz-Josef I. Next door is the "Story of a Fibre", which is dominated by a double-decker costume display: richly embroidered religious vestments above and fashionable attire from the eighteenth century to modern catwalk concoctions below.

"Born in Fire" is home to the museum's impressive glass, ceramic and pottery displays, from eighteenth-century Meissen figures to Art Nouveau Lötz vases. The "Print and Image" room is devoted mainly to Czech photography, and includes numerous prints from the art form's interwar heyday, including several works by František Drtikol, Jaromír Funkes and Josef Sudek. Finally, in the Treasury, there's a kind of modern-day Kunstkammer or cabinet of curiosities: everything from ivory objets d'art and seventeenth-century Italian *pietre dure* (hardstone mosaics) to miniature silver furniture and a goblet made from rhino horn.

to the avant-garde – and its collection is consequently unrivalled. The building itself is richly decorated in mosaics, stained glass and sculptures, and its ground-floor temporary exhibitions are consistently excellent. The permanent collection begins on the first floor with the Votive Hall, which is ornately decorated with trompe-l'oeil wall hangings, lunette paintings and a bewhiskered bust

The Golem

Legends concerning the animation of unformed matter (which is what the Hebrew word **golem** means), using the mystical texts of the Kabbala, were around long before Frankenstein started playing around with corpses. The most famous golem was the giant servant made from the mud of the Vltava by **Rabbi Löw**, the sixteenth-century chief rabbi of Prague, who was brought to life when the rabbi placed a *shem* in its mouth, a tablet with a magic Hebrew inscription.

There are numerous versions of the tale, though none earlier than the nineteenth century. In some, the golem is a figure of fun, flooding the rabbi's kitchen rather in the manner of Disney's *Sorcerer's Apprentice*; others portray him as the guardian of the ghetto, helping Rabbi Löw in his struggle with the anti-Semites at the court of Rudolf II. In almost all versions, however, the golem finally runs amok and Löw has to remove the *shem* once and for all, and hide the creature away in the attic of the Old-New Synagogue, where it has supposedly resided ever since – ready to come out again if needed.

Shops

CHEZ PARISIENNE

Pařížská 8. Mon–Sat 10am–7pm, Sun noon–7pm. MAP P.78, POCKET MAP G11
Prague's sexiest lingerie store takes its name from Prague's most fashion-conscious street Pařížská.

JUDAICA

Široká 7. Daily except Sat 10am–6pm. MAP P.78, POCKET MAP F11
Probably the best stocked of all the places flogging Jewish books to passing tourists, with books and prints, secondhand and new.

JUDAICA

LA BRETAGNE

Široká 22. Mon–Sat 9.30am–7.30pm. MAP P.78, POCKET MAP F11
There's a wide array of fresh fish and seafood at this centrally located fishmonger's, plus takeaway sushi.

Cafés

NOSTRESS

Dušní 10. Daily 10am–midnight. MAP P.78, POCKET MAP G11
Despite the tacky name, this smart, Belgian-owned café is actually a great place in which to unwind amidst the eclectic designer furniture. Decent salads and snacks on offer too.

PANERIA

Kaprova 3. Daily 8am–8pm. MAP P.78, POCKET MAP F11
Central branch of a large chain of Czech bakeries specializing in sandwiches, toasted panini and pastries.

RUDOLFINUM

Alšovo nábřeží 12. Tues–Sun 10am–6pm. MAP P.78, POCKET MAP F11
Gloriously grand nineteenth-century café on the first floor of the old parliament building – you don't have to visit the gallery to go to the café.

Restaurants

LE CAFÉ COLONIAL

Široká 6. ☎ 224 818 322. Daily 10am–midnight. MAP P.78, POCKET MAP F11
Conveniently situated informal café/formal restaurant right opposite the Klausen Synagogue. The colonial theme isn't overplayed, though the vast French-based menu has a touch of Chinese and Indian. Pasta and risotto for under 200Kč; other main courses 200–400Kč.

DINITZ

Bílkova 12. ☎ 222 313 308. Daily except Sat 11.30am–10.30pm. MAP P.78, POCKET MAP G11
Kosher restaurant offering Middle Eastern snacks, sandwiches, pasta, salads (200–250 Kč) and steaks (350–500 Kč).

KING SOLOMON

Široká 8. ☎ 224 818 752. Daily except Fri & Sat noon–11pm. MAP P.78, POCKET MAP F11
Sophisticated kosher restaurant which serves big helpings

LE CAFÉ COLONIAL

of international dishes and traditional Jewish specialities: a three-course set menu (with a beer) will set you back 550Kč.

LES MOULES

Pařížská 19 ☎ 222 315 022. Daily 11.30am–midnight. MAP P.78, POCKET MAP G11

Part of a chain of wood-panelled Belgian brasseries which flies in fresh mussels and serves them up for around 460Kč a kilo, with French fries and Belgian beers.

PIZZERIA RUGANTINO

Dušní 4 ☎ 222 318 172. Mon–Sat 11am–11pm, Sun noon–11pm. MAP P.78, POCKET MAP G11

This pizzeria, just off Dlouhá, is the genuine article: an oak-fired oven, gargantuan thin bases and numerous toppings to choose from (130–220Kč).

PRAVDA (TRUTH)

Pařížská 17 ☎ 222 326 203. Daily noon–1am. MAP P.78, POCKET MAP G11

Chic restaurant with attentive service and an excellent global menu ranging from Cajun to Vietnamese, including home-made pasta dishes and French-style salads. Main dishes hover between 500 and 600Kč.

Pubs and bars

BAROCK

Pařížská 24. Daily 10am–1am. MAP 78, POCKET MAP G11

This is the café-bar of choice for the upwardly mobile locals who shop on fashionable Pařížská – the tagline is the cringe-inducing "delicious meal and beautiful women".

KOLKOVNA

V kolkovně 8. Daily 11am–midnight. MAP P.78, POCKET MAP G11

Justifiably popular with passing tourists, this Pilsner Urquell pub has plush new decor, excellent pub food and unpasteurized Pilsner on tap.

TRETTER'S

V kolkovně 3. Daily 7pm–3am. MAP P.78, POCKET MAP G11

Wonderfully smart and sophisticated (but not exclusive) American cocktail bar, with very professional staff and a celebrity air about the place. Live jazz (Tues).

Venues

DIVADLO IMAGE

Pařížská 4 ☎ 222 329 191, ⓦwww.imagetheatre.cz. Daily 8pm. MAP P.78, POCKET MAP G11

One of the more innovative and entertaining of Prague's ubiquitous venues for "black light theatre" (visual trickery created by "invisible" actors dressed all in black).

RUDOLFINUM

Alšovo nábřeží 12 ☎ 227 059 352, ⓦwww.rudolfinum.cz. MAP P.78, POCKET MAP F11

A truly stunning neo-Renaissance concert hall from the late nineteenth century that's home base for the Czech Philharmonic.

Wenceslas Square and northern Nové Město

Nové Město – Prague's "New Town" – is the city's main commercial and business district, housing most of its big hotels, cinemas, nightclubs, fast-food outlets and department stores. Architecturally, it comes over as big, bourgeois and predominantly *fin de siècle*, yet the large market squares and wide streets were actually laid out way back in the fourteenth century by Emperor Charles IV. The obvious starting point in Nové Město is Wenceslas Square (Václavské náměstí), the long, sloping boulevard with its distinctive, interwar shopping malls, which was at the centre of the 1989 demonstrations against Communism and is today at the hub of the modern city.

WENCESLAS SQUARE (VÁCLAVSKÉ NÁMĚSTÍ)

MAP P.88, POCKET MAP H13–J13

The natural pivot around which modern Prague revolves, **Wenceslas Square** is more of a wide, gently sloping boulevard than a square as such. It's scarcely a conventional – or even convenient – space in which to hold mass demonstrations, yet for the past 150 years or more it has been the focus of political protest in Prague. In August 1968 it was the scene of some of the most violent confrontations between the Soviet invaders and the local Czechs. More happily, in late November 1989, more than 250,000 people crammed into the square night after night, often enduring subzero temperatures, to demand free elections.

Despite the square's history and its medieval origins, it is now a thoroughly modern, glitzy, slightly seedy boulevard, lined with self-important six- or seven-storey buildings representing every artistic trend of the last hundred years, from neo-Renaissance to Socialist Realism. At the top of the square, in front of the grandiose National Museum, stands the **Wenceslas Monument**, a worthy and heroic, but pretty unexciting, equestrian statue of the country's patron saint. Below the statue, a simple memorial commemorating the victims of Communism is adorned with flowers and photos of Jan Palach and Jan

Zajíc, both of whom martyred themselves here in 1969 in protest at the Soviet invasion.

LUCERNA

MAP P.88, POCKET MAP H14

Wenceslas Square has an impressive array of old shopping arcades, or *pasáže*, as they're known in Czech, mostly dating from the interwar period. The king of the lot is the lavishly decorated *fin de siècle* **Lucerna pasáž**, stretching all the way from Štěpánská to Vodičkova. Designed in the early part of the twentieth century in Moorish style by, among others, Václav Havel's own grandfather, it boasts an ornate cinema, café and vast concert hall. Suspended from the ceiling in the centre of the arcade is David Černý's parody of the square's equestrian Wenceslas Monument, with the saint astride an upside-down charger.

NATIONAL MUSEUM (NÁRODNÍ MUZEUM)

Václavské náměstí 68 ⓦ www.nm.cz. Mon–Fri 10am–6pm, Sat 10am–8pm, Sun 11am–7pm. Closed first Tues of month. 150Kč. MAP P.88, POCKET MAP J14

Built in 1890, the broad, brooding hulk of the **National Museum** dominates the view up Wenceslas Square like a giant golden eagle with outstretched wings. It's worth taking at least a quick look at the ornate marble entrance hall and splendid monumental staircase leading to the glass-domed Pantheon, with its 48 busts and statues of distinguished bewhiskered Czech men (plus a couple of token women and Slovaks). The rest of the vast permanent collection is dowdy, poorly labelled and filled with coins, fossils and stuffed animals. The museum's temporary exhibitions can be very good, though, so it's always worth checking to see what's on.

PRAGUE MAIN TRAIN STATION (PRAHA HLAVNÍ NÁDRAŽÍ

MAP P.88, POCKET MAP K13

Prague's main train station is one of the final architectural glories of the dying Habsburg Empire, designed by **Josef Fanta** and officially opened in 1909 as the Franz-Josefs Bahnhof. Arriving by metro, or buying tickets in the over-polished subterranean modern section, it's easy to miss the station's surviving Art Nouveau parts. Upstairs, the original entrance – now blighted by a motorway outside – still exudes imperial confidence, with its wrought-iron canopy and naked figurines clinging to the sides of the towers.

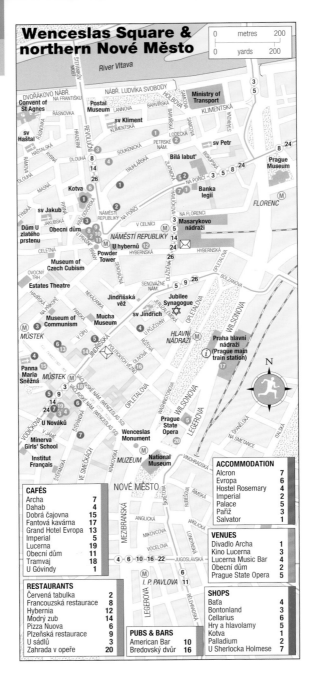

Wenceslas Square & northern Nové Město

| | 0 | metres | 200 |
| | 0 | yards | 200 |

CAFÉS

Archa	7
Dahab	4
Dobrá čajovna	15
Fantová kavárna	17
Grand Hotel Evropa	13
Imperial	5
Lucerna	19
Obecní dům	11
Tramvaj	18
U Góvindy	1

RESTAURANTS

Červená tabulka	2
Francouzská restaurace	8
Hybernia	12
Modrý zub	14
Pizza Nuova	6
Plzeňská restaurace	9
U sádlů	3
Zahrada v opeře	20

PUBS & BARS

American Bar	10
Bredovský dvůr	16

ACCOMMODATION

Alcron	7
Evropa	6
Hostel Rosemary	4
Imperial	2
Palace	5
Paříž	3
Salvator	1

VENUES

Divadlo Archa	1
Kino Lucerna	3
Lucerna Music Bar	4
Obecní dům	2
Prague State Opera	5

SHOPS

Baťa	4
Bontonland	3
Cellarius	6
Hry a hlavolamy	5
Kotva	1
Palladium	2
U Sherlocka Holmese	7

JUBILEE SYNAGOGUE

Jeruzalémská. April–Oct daily except Sat 11am–5pm. 80Kč. MAP OPPOSITE, POCKET MAP J12

Named in honour of the sixtieth year of the Emperor Franz-Josef I's reign in 1908, the **Jubilee Synagogue** was built in an incredibly colourful Moorish style similar to that of the Spanish Synagogue in Josefov, but with a touch of Art Nouveau. The Hebrew quote from Malachi on the facade strikes a note of liberal optimism: "Do we not have one father? Were we not created by the same God?"

JINDŘIŠSKÁ VĚŽ

MAP OPPOSITE, POCKET MAP J12

This freestanding fifteenth-century tower is the belfry of the nearby church of **sv Jindřich** (St Henry), whose digitally controlled, high-pitched bells ring out every fifteen minutes, and play an entire medley every four hours. In contrast to every other surviving tower in Prague, the **Jindřišská věž** has been imaginatively and expensively restored and now contains a café, restaurant, shop, exhibition space and, on the top floor, a small **museum** (April–Oct Mon–Fri 9am–7pm, Sat & Sun 10am–7pm; Oct–March closes 6pm; 60Kč) on Prague's hundred-plus towers, with a good view across the city's rooftops.

MUCHA MUSEUM

Panská 7 ⓦ www.mucha.cz. Daily 10am–6pm. 120Kč. MAP OPPOSITE, POCKET MAP H12-13

Alfons Mucha (1860–1939) made his name in *fin de siècle* Paris, where he shot to fame after designing Art Nouveau posters for the actress Sarah Bernhardt. "Le Style Mucha" became all the rage, but the artist himself came to despise this "commercial" period of his work, and, in 1910, Mucha moved back to his homeland and threw himself into the national cause, designing patriotic stamps, banknotes and posters for the new republic. The whole of Mucha's career is covered in the permanent exhibition, and an excellent video (in English) covers the decade of his life he devoted to the cycle of nationalist paintings known as the Slav Epic.

MUSEUM OF COMMUNISM (MUZEUM KOMUNISMU)

Na příkopě 10 ⓦ www.muzeumkomunismu .cz. Daily 9am–9pm. 180Kč. MAP OPPOSITE, POCKET MAP H12

Above a casino, on the first floor of the Savarin Palace, the **Museum of Communism** gives a brief rundown of Czech twentieth-century history, accompanied by a superb collection of Communist statues, film footage and propaganda posters. The politics are a bit simplistic – the popular postwar support for the Party is underplayed – but it's worth tracking down for the memorabilia alone.

JUBILEE SYNAGOGUE

POWDER TOWER (PRAŠNÁ BRÁNA)

Daily April–Oct 10am–6pm. 70Kč. MAP P.88,
POCKET MAP H12

One of the eight medieval gate-towers that once guarded Staré Město, the Powder Tower was begun by King Vladislav Jagiello in 1475, shortly after he'd moved into the royal court, which was situated next door at the time. Work stopped when he retreated to the Hrad to avoid the wrath of his subjects; later on, it was used to store gunpowder – hence the name and the reason for the damage incurred in 1757, when it blew up. Most people, though, ignore the small historical exhibition inside, and climb straight up for the modest view from the top.

OBECNÍ DŮM (MUNICIPAL HOUSE)

Náměstí Republiky 5 ⓦ www.obecni-dum.cz.
MAP P.88, POCKET MAP H11–12

Attached to the Powder Tower, and built on the ruins of the old royal court, the **Obecní dům** is by far the most exciting Art Nouveau building in Prague, one of the few places that still manages to conjure up the atmosphere of Prague's turn-of-the-twentieth-century café society. Conceived as a cultural centre for the Czech community, it's probably the finest architectural achievement of the Czech national revival, extravagantly decorated inside and out by the leading Czech artists of the day. From the lifts to the cloakrooms, just about all the furnishings remain as they were when the building was completed in 1911.

The simplest way of soaking up the interior – peppered with mosaics and pendulous brass chandeliers – is to have a coffee in the cavernous **café** (see p.93). For a more detailed inspection of the building's spectacular interior, you can sign up for one of the regular **guided tours** at the information centre (daily 10am–7pm; 270Kč) on the ground floor.

BANKA LEGIÍ

Na poříčí 24. Mon–Fri 9am–5pm. Free.
MAP P.88, POCKET MAP J11

The **Banka legií** (now a branch of the ČSOB) is one of Prague's most unusual pieces of corporate architecture. A Rondo-Cubist building from the early 1920s, it boasts a striking white marble frieze by Otto Gutfreund, depicting the epic march across

OBECNÍ DŮM

FRIEZE ON THE BANKA LEGII

Siberia undertaken by the Czechoslovak Legion and their embroilment in the Russian Revolution, set into the bold smoky-red moulding of the facade. You're free to wander into the main banking hall on the ground floor, which retains its curved glass roof and distinctive red-and-white marble patterning.

PRAGUE MUSEUM

Na poříčí 52 🌐 www.muzeumprahy.cz. Tues–Sun 9am–6pm. 100Kč. MAP P.88, POCKET MAP K11/F5

A purpose-built neo-Renaissance mansion next to a noisy motorway houses the **Prague Museum**. Inside, there's an ad hoc collection of the city's art, a number of antique bicycles, and usually an intriguing temporary exhibition on some aspect of the city. The museum's prize possession, though, is Antonín Langweil's paper model of Prague which he completed in the 1830s. It's a fascinating insight into early nineteenth-century Prague – predominantly Baroque, with the cathedral incomplete and the Jewish quarter "unsanitized" – and, consequently, has served as one of the most useful records for the city's restorers. The most

surprising thing, of course, is that so little has changed.

POSTAL MUSEUM (POŠTOVNÍ MUZEUM)

Nové mlýny 2. Tues–Sun 9am–noon & 1–5pm. 25Kč. MAP P.88, POCKET MAP J10

Housed in the **Vávrův dům**, an old mill near one of Prague's many water towers, the **Postal Museum** contains a series of jolly nineteenth-century wall paintings of Romantic Austrian landscapes, and a collection of drawings on postman themes. The real philately is on the ground floor – a vast international collection of stamps arranged in vertical pull-out drawers. The Czechoslovak issues are historically and artistically interesting, as well as of appeal to collectors. Stamps became a useful tool in the propaganda wars of the last century; even such short-lived ventures as the Hungarian-backed Slovak Soviet Republic of 1918–19 and the Slovak National Uprising of autumn 1944 managed to print special issues. Under the First Republic, the country's leading artists, notably Alfons Mucha and Max Švabinský, were commissioned to design stamps, some of which are exceptionally beautiful.

Shops

BAŤA

Václavské náměstí 6. Mon–Fri 9am–9pm, Sat 9am–8pm, Sun 10am–8pm. MAP P.88, POCKET MAP H13

Functionalist flagship store of Baťa shoe empire with five floors of fancy footwear in a prime position on Wenceslas Square.

BONTONLAND

Václavské náměstí 1. Mon–Sat 9am–8pm, Sun 10am–7pm. MAP P.88, POCKET MAP H13

In the *pasáž* at the bottom of Wenceslas Square, this is Prague's biggest record store, with three floors of rock, folk, jazz and classical CDs, DVDs and video games.

CELLARIUS

Štěpánská 61. Mon–Sat 9.30am–9pm, Sun 3–8pm. MAP P.88, POCKET MAP H13

Very well-stocked shop in the Lucerna *pasáž*, where you can taste and take away Czech wines.

HRY A HLAVOLAMY

Václavské náměstí 38. Mon–Fri 10am–7pm, Sat & Sun 11am–5pm. MAP P.88, POCKET MAP H13

A small shop inside the Rokoko *pasáž* which stocks some great wooden puzzles and brainteasers (*hlavolamy*), plus board games.

KOTVA

Náměstí Republiky 8. Mon–Fri 9am–8pm, Sat 10am–7pm, Sun 10am–6pm. MAP P.88, POCKET MAP H11

A seminal piece of dreadful brown 1970s architecture, Kotva is a good old-fashioned Czech department store, with prices to suit all pockets.

PALLADIUM

Náměstí Republiky 1. Mon–Fri 7am–10pm, Sat & Sun 8am–10pm. MAP P.88, POCKET MAP J11

The apotheosis of Czech consumerism, this is the country's largest shopping mall, and it occupies the spruced-up former barracks opposite Obecní dům.

U SHERLOCKA HOLMESE

Vodičkova 38. Daily 6am–11pm. MAP P.88, POCKET MAP H14

This calls itself a "cigar and pipe shop", but you'll find other sorts of smoking paraphernalia here too, plus plenty of bottles of spirits, including absinthe.

Cafés

ARCHA

Na poříčí 26. Mon–Fri 9am–10.30pm, Sat 10am–10pm, Sun noon–10pm. MAP P.88, POCKET MAP J11

Designer café-bar belonging to the Prague's cutting-edge theatre venue of the same name, with big fishbowl windows for people-watching. Light snacks only; free wi-fi.

DAHAB

Soukenická 4. Mon–Fri 11am–1am, Sat 2pm–3am, Sun 2pm–midnight. MAP P.88, POCKET MAP J11

Dahab gives you the full harem monty, with drapery galore, cushions and carpets, hookahs, plus Middle Eastern snacks.

IMPERIAL CAFÉ

DOBRÁ ČAJOVNA

Václavské náměstí 14. Mon–Fri 10am–9.30pm, Sat & Sun 2–9.30pm. MAP P.88, POCKET MAP H13

Mellow, rarefied teahouse, with an astonishing variety of teas (and a few Middle Eastern snacks) served by waiters who slip by silently in their sandals.

FANTOVÁ KAVÁRNA

Praha hlavní nádraží. Daily 6am–11pm. MAP P.88, POCKET MAP K13

The café is situated in the rundown former ticket hall in the Art Nouveau section of the main train station – it's also worth taking a peek at the ceramic pillars in the former station restaurant.

GRAND HOTEL EVROPA

Václavské náměstí 25. Daily 9.30am–11pm. MAP P.88, POCKET MAP H13

This sumptuous Art Nouveau café has all its original fittings, but has reached a new low in ambience and service. For architectural curiosity only.

IMPERIAL

Na poříčí 15. Daily 7am–11pm. MAP P.88, POCKET MAP J11

Built in 1914, and featuring the most incredible ceramic friezes on its walls, pillars and ceilings, the *Imperial* is a must for fans of outrageously sumptuous Art Nouveau decor. You can just come for a coffee, but they also serve breakfast, light lunches and full-on main dishes for 300Kč or so.

LUCERNA

Vodičkova 36. Daily 10am–midnight. MAP P.88, POCKET MAP H14

Wonderfully lugubrious *fin de siècle* café-bar on the first floor, en route to the cinema of the same name, with lots of faux marble and windows overlooking the Lucerna *pasáž*.

OBECNÍ DŮM

Náměstí Republiky 5. Daily 7.30am–11pm. MAP P.88, POCKET MAP H11-12

The vast *kavárna*, with its famous fountain, is a glittering Art Nouveau period piece. Food is nice enough, but most folk come here for a coffee and a little something from the cake trolley.

TRAMVAJ

Václavské náměstí. Mon–Sat 9am–midnight, Sun 10am–midnight. MAP P.88, POCKET MAP H13

Two vintage no. 11 trams stranded in the middle of Wenceslas Square (where they used to run) have been converted into a café – a convenient spot for coffee, and easy to locate.

U GÓVINDY

Soukenická 27. Mon–Sat noon–5pm. MAP P.88, POCKET MAP J10

Daytime Hare Krishna (Haré Kršna in Czech) restaurant with very basic decor, serving organic Indian veggie dishes for just 85Kč.

CAFÉ TRAMVAJ

Restaurants

ČERVENÁ TABULKA (RED TABLET)

Lodecká 4 ☎ 224 810 401. Daily 11.30am–11pm. MAP P.88, POCKET MAP J10

Famed for its duck in gingerbread sauce and its wide choice of fish and seafood, this little villa restaurant delivers attentive service and has a slightly offbeat, cosy interior. Mains 300–450Kč.

FRANCOUZSKÁ RESTAURACE

Obecní dům, Náměstí Republiky 5 ☎ 222 002 770. Daily 11.30am–4pm & 6–11pm. MAP P.88, POCKET MAP H11

The Art Nouveau decor in this cavernous Obecní dům restaurant is stunning and the French-style main dishes (300–600Kč) are superb.

HYBERNIA

Hybernská 7 ☎ 222 226 004. Mon–Fri 8am–11.30pm, Sat & Sun 10.30am–11.30pm. MAP P.88, POCKET MAP J12

Busy restaurant, with a nice outdoor terrace out the back; specializes in *špízy* (needles), aka kebabs, but also serves good-value Czech food and pasta dishes (150–350Kč).

MODRÝ ZUB (BLUE TOOTH)

Jindřišská 5 ☎ 222 212 622. Daily 11am–11pm. MAP P.88, POCKET MAP H13

Good-value Thai rice and noodle dishes (175–275Kč) in a place that has a modern wine-bar feel to it – popular with Wenceslas Square shoppers.

PIZZA NUOVA

Revoluční 1 ☎ 222 803 308. Daily 11.30am–11.30pm. MAP P.88, POCKET MAP H11

Big, spacious, stylish upstairs pizza and pasta place, with great views of the trams wending their way through náměstí Republiky. Pizzas go for around 200Kč; pasta dishes for a little less.

PLZEŇSKÁ RESTAURACE

Obecní dům, Náměstí Republiky 5 ☎ 222 002 770, ⊕ www.obecni-dum.cz. Daily 11am–11pm. MAP P.88, POCKET MAP H11

Decent Czech beer hall-restaurant in the cellar of the Obecní dům, cheaper than the *Francouzská restaurace* upstairs (main dishes 250–400Kč), but not quite the same aesthetic experience.

U SÁDLŮ (THE LARD)

Klimentská 2. Daily 11am–11.30pm. MAP P.88, POCKET MAP H11

Deliberately over-the-top themed medieval banqueting hall offering a hearty Czech menu, with classics such as roast pork knuckle and goulash (200–400Kč) helped down with lashings of frothing Budvar.

PRAGUE STATE OPERA

ZAHRADA V OPEŘE (OPERA GARDEN)

Legerova 75 ☎ 224 239 685. Daily 11.30am–1am. MAP P.88, POCKET MAP J14
Striking modern interior and beautifully presented food from around the world at democratic prices. Huge salads for just 150Kč; main dishes for 200–500Kč; and creative desserts for 125Kč. Free wi-fi.

Pubs and bars

AMERICAN BAR

Obecní dům, Náměstí Republiky 5. Daily 11am–11pm. MAP P.88, POCKET MAP H12
Underused and pricey, the bar in the basement of the Obecní dům is nevertheless another architectural treat from 1911.

BREDOVSKÝ DVŮR

Politických vězňů 12. Mon–Sat 11am–midnight, Sun 11am–11pm. MAP P.88, POCKET MAP J13
Popular, brick-vaulted city pub, off Wenceslas Square, serving standard pub food washed down with Pilsner Urquell or Velkopopovický kozel.

Venues

DIVADLO ARCHA

Na poříčí 26 ☎ 221 716 333, Ⓦ www.archatheatre.cz. MAP P.88, POCKET MAP J11
By far the most innovative venue in Prague, with two versatile spaces, an art gallery and a café. The programme includes music, dance and theatre with an emphasis on new and experimental work. English subtitles or translation often available.

KINO LUCERNA

Vodičkova 36 ☎ 224 216 972, Ⓦ www.lucerna.cz. MAP P.88, POCKET MAP H14
Grandiose, gilded 1909 cinema

OBECNÍ DŮM CONCERT HALL

that eschews dubbed films and often shows Czech films with English subtitles.

LUCERNA MUSIC BAR

Vodičkova 36 ☎ 224 217 108, Ⓦ www.musicbar.cz. Daily 8pm–3am. MAP P.88, POCKET MAP H14
Scruffy basement bar that attracts some great musicians, local and touring, during the week before descending into pop disco at the weekend. Cover 80Kč and upwards.

OBECNÍ DŮM – SMETANOVA SÍŇ

Náměstí Republiky 5 ☎ 222 002336, Ⓦ www.obecni-dum.cz. MAP P.88, POCKET MAP H12
Fantastically ornate Art Nouveau concert hall which usually kicks off the Prague Spring festival and is home to the excellent Prague Symphony Orchestra.

PRAGUE STATE OPERA (STÁTNÍ OPERA PRAHA)

Wilsonova 4 ☎ 224 227 266, Ⓦ www.opera.cz. MAP P.88, POCKET MAP J14
A sumptuous nineteenth-century opera house, originally built by the city's German-speaking community. It's now the number-two venue for opera, with a repertoire that tends to focus on Italian works.

Národní and southern Nové Město

Off the conventional tourist trail, and boasting only a few minor sights, the network of cobbled streets immediately to the south of Národní is nevertheless great to explore, as it harbours a whole range of interesting cafés, pubs, restaurants and shops that have steadily colonized the area over the past two decades. Southern Nové Město also boasts the city's finest stretch of waterfront, with a couple of leafy islands overlooked by magnificent *fin de siècle* mansions that continue almost without interruption south to Vyšehrad.

JUNGMANNOVO NÁMĚSTÍ

MAP OPPOSITE, POCKET MAP G13

Jungmannovo náměstí is named for **Josef Jungmann** (1772–1847), a prolific writer, translator and leading light of the Czech national revival, whose pensive, seated statue surveys the small, ill-proportioned square. The square itself boasts a couple of Czech architectural curiosities, starting with a unique **Cubist streetlamp** (and seat) from 1912, in the far eastern corner. The most imposing building is the chunky, vigorously sculptured

Palác Adria, designed in Rondo-Cubist style in the early 1920s, with sculptural extras by Otto Gutfreund and a central *Seafaring* group by Jan Štursa. The building's *pasáž* (arcade) still retains its wonderful original portal featuring sculptures depicting the twelve signs of the zodiac. The theatre in the basement was the underground nerve centre of the 1989 Velvet Revolution, where the Civic Forum thrashed out tactics in the dressing rooms and gave daily press conferences in the auditorium against the stage set for Dürenmatt's *Minotaurus*.

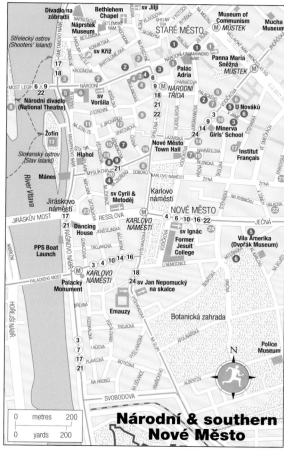

**Národní & southern
Nové Město**

| metres | 200 |
| yards | 200 |

RESTAURANTS	
Cicala	21
Čínská restaurace po sečuánsku	2
Dynamo	11
Lemon Leaf	20
Pizzeria Kmotra	12
Posezení u Čiriny	19
Střelecký ostrov	8
Žofín Garden	13

SHOPS	
Globe	8
Gold Pralines	6
Jan Pazdera	5
Le Patio	4
MPM	9
Music Antikvariát	2
My národní	3
Quasimodo Vintage Fashion	1
Včelařské Potřeby	7

PUBS & BARS	
Branický sklípek	10
Novoměstský pivovar	14
Pivovarský dům	24
Potrefená husa	23
U Fleků	15
U havrana	22
U kruhu	7
U Pinkasů	1

CLUBS & VENUES	
Divadlo Minor	7
Evald	1
Laterna magika	6
MAT Studio	8
N11	2
National Theatre	5
Reduta	3
Rock Café	4

CAFÉS	
Café 35	17
Globe	18
Louvre	4
Marathon	16
St Tropez	6
Shabu	5
Slavia	3
Velryba	9

ACCOMMODATION	
Hotel 16 – U sv Kateřiny	6
Icon Hotel	3
Klub Habitat	4
Miss Sophie's	5
Na zlatém kříži	1
U Šuterů	2

CHURCH OF PANNA MARIA SNĚŽNÁ

Jungmannovo náměstí 18. MAP P.97.
POCKET MAP H13

Once one of the great landmarks of Wenceslas Square, **Panna Maria Sněžná** (St Mary-of-the-Snows) is now barely visible from the surrounding streets. To reach the church, go through the archway behind the statue of Jungmann, and across the courtyard beyond. Founded in the fourteenth century as a Carmelite monastery by Emperor Charles IV, who envisaged a vast coronation church larger than St Vitus Cathedral, only the chancel got built before the money ran out. The result is curious – a church which is short in length, but equal to the cathedral in height. The 33-metre-high, prettily painted vaulting is awesome, as is the gargantuan gold and black Baroque main altar which almost touches the ceiling.

NÁRODNÍ

MAP P.97, POCKET MAP F14–G13

It was on this busy street, lined with shops, galleries and clubs, that the Velvet Revolution began. On **November 17, 1989**, a 50,000-strong student demonstration worked its way down Národní aiming to reach Wenceslas Square. Halfway down the street their way was barred by the Communist riot-police. The students sat down and refused to disperse, some of them handing flowers out to the police. Suddenly, without any warning, the police attacked, and what became known as the *masakr* (massacre) began. In actual fact, no one was killed, though it wasn't for want of trying by the police. Under the arches of Národní 16, there's a small symbolic bronze relief of eight hands reaching out for help.

Further down Národní, on the right-hand side, is an eye-catching duo of Art Nouveau buildings. The first, at no. 7, was built for the **Prague Savings Bank** (**pojišťovna Praha**), hence the beautiful mosaic lettering above the windows advertising *život* (life insurance) and *kapital* (loans), as well as help with your *důchod* (pension) and *věno* (dowry). Next door, the slightly more ostentatious **Topičův dům**, headquarters of the official state publishers, provides the perfect accompaniment, with a similarly ornate wrought-iron and glass canopy.

CAFÉ SLAVIA

Smetanovo nábřeží 2. Daily 9am–11pm.
MAP P.97, POCKET MAP F13

The **Café Slavia**, opposite the National Theatre, has been a favourite haunt of the city's writers, dissidents, artists and actors since the 1920s when the Czech avant-garde movement, **Devětsil**, used to hold its meetings here, recorded for posterity by Nobel prize-winning poet Jaroslav Seifert. Under the Communists, dissident (and later president) Václav Havel and his pals used to hang out here. The ambience

MEMORIAL SCULPTURE ON NÁRODNÍ

17.11.1989

is not what it once was, but it still has a great riverside view and Viktor Oliva's classic *Absinthe Drinker* canvas on the wall.

STŘELECKÝ OSTROV (SHOOTERS' ISLAND)

Most Legií. MAP P.97, POCKET MAP E13–14

The **Střelecký ostrov** is where the army held their shooting practice, on and off, from the fifteenth until the nineteenth century. Closer to the other bank, and accessible via **most Legií** (Legion's Bridge), it became a favourite spot for a Sunday promenade, and is still popular, especially in summer. The first Sokol gymnastics festival was held here in 1882 and the first May Day demonstrations took place here in 1890.

NATIONAL THEATRE (NÁRODNÍ DIVADLO)

Národní 2 ⊕ www.narodni-divadlo.cz. MAP P.97, POCKET MAP F14

Overlooking the Vltava is the gold-crested **National Theatre**, proud symbol of the Czech nation. Refused money from the Habsburg state coffers, Czechs of all classes dug deep into their pockets to raise the funds. After thirteen years of construction, in June 1881, the theatre opened with a premiere of Smetana's *Libuše*. In August of the same year, fire ripped through the building, destroying everything except the outer walls. Within two years the whole thing was rebuilt and even the emperor contributed this time. The grand portal on the north side of the theatre is embellished with suitably triumphant allegorical figures, and, inside, every square centimetre is taken up with paintings and sculptures by leading artists of the Czech national revival.

Standing behind the old National Theatre, and in dramatic contrast with it, is the theatre's state-of-the-art extension, the opaque glass box of the **Nová scéna**, completed in 1983. It's one of those buildings most Praguers love to hate, though compared to much of Prague's Communist-era architecture, it's not that bad. Just for the record, the lump of molten rock in the courtyard is a symbolic evocation entitled *My Socialist Country*.

U NOVÁKŮ ON VODIČKOVA

VODIČKOVA

MAP P.97, POCKET MAP G14–H13

Vodičkova is probably the most impressive of the streets that head south from Wenceslas Square. Of the handful of buildings worth checking out on the way, the most remarkable is **U Nováků** with its mosaic of bucolic frolicking and its delicate, ivy-like wrought-ironwork – look out for the frog-prince holding up a windowsill. Further down the street stands the imposing neo-Renaissance **Minerva** girls' school, covered in bright red sgraffito. Founded in 1866, it was the first such institution in Prague, and was notorious for the antics of its pupils, the "Minervans", who shocked bourgeois Czech society with their experimentation with fashion, drugs and sexual freedom.

KARLOVO NÁMĚSTÍ

MAP P.97, POCKET MAP G15

Once Prague's biggest square, **Karlovo náměstí**'s impressive proportions are no longer so easy to appreciate, obscured by trees and cut in two by a busy thoroughfare. It was created by Emperor Charles IV as Nové Město's cattle market and used by him for the grisly annual public display of his impressive collection of saintly relics. Now it signals the southern limit of the city's main commercial district and the beginning of predominantly residential Nové Město.

NOVÉ MĚSTO TOWN HALL (NOVOMĚSTSKÁ RADNICE)

Karlovo náměstí 23 ⓦ www .novomestskaradnice.cz. Easter to mid-Oct daily 10am–6pm. 50Kč. MAP P.97, POCKET MAP G14

Built in the fourteenth century, the **Nové Město Town Hall** is one of the finest Gothic buildings in the city, sporting three impressive triangular gables embellished with intricate blind tracery. It was here that Prague's **first defenestration** took place on July 30, 1419, when the radical Hussite preacher Jan Želivský and his penniless religious followers stormed the building, mobbed the councillors and burghers, and threw twelve or thirteen of them (including the mayor) out of the town hall windows onto the pikes of the Hussite mob below, who clubbed any survivors to death. Václav IV, on hearing the news, suffered a stroke and died just two weeks later. So began the long and bloody Hussite Wars. After the amalgamation of Prague's separate towns in 1784, the building was used solely as a criminal court and prison. Nowadays, you can visit the site of the defenestration, and climb to the top of the tower for a view over central Prague. The town hall also puts on temporary art exhibitions.

CHURCH OF SV IGNÁC

Karlovo náměstí. MAP P.97, POCKET MAP G15
Begun in 1665, this former **Jesuit church** is quite remarkable inside, a pink and white confection, with lots of frothy stucco work and an exuberant pulpit dripping with gold drapery, cherubs and saints. The statue of St Ignatius, which sits above the entrance surrounded by a sunburst, caused controversy at the time, as until then only the Holy Trinity had been depicted in such a way.

CATHEDRAL OF SV CYRIL AND METODĚJ (HEYDRICH MARTYRS' MONUMENT)

Resslova/Na Zderaze. Tues–Sun: March–Oct 10am–5pm; Nov–Feb 10am–4pm. 60Kč.
MAP P.97, POCKET MAP F15
Amid all the traffic, it's extremely difficult to imagine the scene outside Prague's **Orthodox cathedral** on June 18, 1942, when seven Czechoslovak secret agents were besieged in the church by hundreds of SS troops. The agents had pulled off the dramatic assassination of Nazi leader **Reinhard Heydrich**, but had been betrayed by one of their own men. The Nazis surrounded the church just after 4am and fought a pitched battle for over six hours, trying explosives, flooding and any other method they could think of to drive the men out of their stronghold in the crypt. Eventually, all seven agents committed suicide rather than give themselves up. There's a plaque at street level on the south wall commemorating those who died, and an exhibition inside – you can also visit the crypt itself, which has been left pretty much as it was.

SLOVANSKÝ OSTROV (SLAV ISLAND)

Masarykovo nábřeží. MAP P.97, POCKET MAP E14–F15
Slovanský ostrov is commonly known as **Žofín**, after the island's very yellow cultural centre, built in 1835 and named for Sophie, the mother of Emperor Franz-Josef I. By the late nineteenth century the island had become one of the city's foremost pleasure gardens, and even today concerts, balls and other social gatherings take place here. Rowing boats can be rented in the summer and there's a boat service between the island and the shore. At the island's southern tip stands the onion-domed **Šítek water tower** and, spanning the narrow channel between the island and the embankment, the **Mánes** art gallery (Tues–Sun 10am–6pm), a striking, white functionalist box designed in 1930.

NOVÉ MĚSTO TOWN HALL

NÁRODNÍ AND SOUTHERN NOVÉ MĚSTO

DANCING HOUSE (TANČÍCÍ DŮM)

Rašínovo nábřeží 80. MAP P.97, POCKET MAP F15

Designed by Frank O. Gehry and Vlado Milunič, this building is known as the **Dancing House** (Tančící dům) or "Fred and Ginger building", after the shape of the building's two towers, which look vaguely like a couple ballroom dancing. The apartment block next door was built at the start of the twentieth century by Havel's grandfather, and was where, until the early 1990s, Havel and his first wife, Olga, lived in the top-floor flat.

PALACKÝ MONUMENT

Palackého náměstí. MAP P.97, POCKET MAP D7

The **Monument to František Palacký**, the nineteenth-century Czech historian, politician and nationalist, is an energetic and inspirational Art Nouveau sculpture from 1912. Ethereal bronze bodies, representing the world of the imagination, shoot out at all angles, contrasting sharply with the plain stone mass of the plinth, and below, the giant seated figure of Palacký, representing the real world.

EMAUZY MONASTERY

Vyšehradská 49 ⓦ www.emauzy.cz. June–Sept Mon–Sat 11am–5pm; Oct–May Mon–Fri 11am–5pm. 30Kč. MAP P.97, POCKET MAP D8

The intertwined concrete spires of the **Emauzy monastery** are an unusual modern addition to the Prague skyline. The monastery was one of the few important historical buildings to be damaged in World War II, in this case by a stray Anglo–American bomb (the pilot thought he was over Dresden). Founded by Emperor Charles IV, the cloisters contain some extremely valuable Gothic frescoes.

DANCING HOUSE

Shops

GLOBE

Pštrossova 6. Daily 9.30am–1am. MAP P.97,
POCKET MAP F15

The expat bookstore *par
excellence* – both a social centre
and superbly well-stocked
store, with an adjacent café and
friendly staff.

GOLD PRALINES

V jámě 5. Mon–Fri 9am–8pm, Sat & Sun
9am–6pm. MAP P.97, POCKET MAP H14

Top quality Belgian chocolates
– make sure you try the
uniquely Czech pralines filled
with the national *digestif*,
Becherovka.

JAN PAZDERA

Vodičkova 28. Mon–Fri 10am–6pm. MAP P.97,
POCKET MAP H14

Truly spectacular selection
of old and new cameras,
microscopes, telescopes, opera
glasses and binoculars.

LE PATIO

Národní 22. Mon–Fri 8am–7pm, Sat & Sun
10am–11pm. MAP P.97, POCKET MAP G13

Stylish café-restaurant that also
sells its furnishings from the
chairs and chandeliers to the
bottle-racks and birdcages.

MPM

Myslíkova 19. Mon–Fri 10am–6pm. MAP P.97,
POCKET MAP F15

A whole range of kits for
making model planes, tanks,
trains, ships and cars, and toy
soldiers.

MUSIC ANTIKVARIÁT

Národní 25. Mon–Sat 10.30am–7pm. MAP P.97,
POCKET MAP F13

The best secondhand record
store in Prague, particularly
good for jazz and folk, but also
rock/pop – though there's not
much in the way of classical.

GLOBE BOOKSTORE

MY NÁRODNÍ

Národní 26. Mon–Sat 7am–9pm, Sun
8am–8pm. MAP P.97, POCKET MAP G13

My Národní is Prague's premier
downtown department store.
The name is a pun on its
Communist predecessor (called
Máj), and it's actually owned
by British supermarket chain
Tesco, as the basement food
hall attests.

QUASIMODO VINTAGE FASHION

Vladislavova 17. Mon–Fri 10am–6pm. MAP P.97,
POCKET MAP G13

Good secondhand store hidden
away in an attractive courtyard.
The clothes and accessories
here are not exclusively vintage,
more plain old secondhand,
and all the more affordable
for it, with pieces around
200–400Kč.

VČELAŘSKÉ POTŘEBY

Křemencova 8. Mon & Wed 9am–5pm, Tues
& Thurs 9am–6pm, Fri 9am–2pm. MAP P.97
POCKET MAP F14.

This shop is a beekeeper's
paradise, with all the
accoutrements required by an
apiarist. It also stocks a wide
selection of delicious honey.

Cafés

CAFÉ 35 – INSTITUT FRANÇAIS

Štěpánská 35. Mon & Fri 8.30am–8pm, Sat 10am–2pm. MAP P.97, POCKET MAP H14

Housed in Prague's Institut Français, you can be sure of great coffee and fresh French pastries – plus of course the chance to pose with a French newspaper. Free wi-fi.

GLOBE

Pštrossova 6. Daily 9.30am–1am. MAP P.97, POCKET MAP F15

Large, buzzing café, at the back of the English-language bookstore of the same name that's a popular expat hang-out, but enjoyable nevertheless, with live music on Friday and Saturday evenings. Free wi-fi and terminals available at 1Kč/minute.

LOUVRE

Národní 22. Mon–Fri 8am–11.30pm, Sat & Sun 9am–11.30pm. MAP P.97, POCKET MAP G13

Early twentieth-century café with a long pedigree, and still a very popular refuelling spot for Prague's shoppers. Dodgy colour scheme, but high ceiling, mirrors, daily papers, decent, inexpensive food, lots of cakes, a billiard hall and window seats overlooking Národní.

MARATHON CAFÉ

MARATHON

Černá 9. Mon–Fri 10am–10pm. MAP P.97, POCKET MAP G14

Smoky, self-styled "library café" in the university's 1920s-style religious faculty, hidden in the backstreets, south of Národní.

ST TROPEZ

Vodičkova 30. Mon–Fri 8am–7pm, Sat & Sun 9.30am–7pm. MAP P.97, POCKET MAP H14

Light and airy, family-run French patisserie inside the U Nováků building on Vodičkova.

SHABU

Palackého 11. Daily 11am–11pm. MAP P.97, POCKET MAP H14

Tiny little café down a passageway, serving an interesting selection of Balkan snacks such as grilled aubergine and *burek*.

SLAVIA

Smetanovo nábřeží 2. Daily 9am–11pm. MAP P.97, POCKET MAP F13

This famous 1920s riverside café pulls in a mixed crowd from shoppers and tourists to old-timers and the pre- and post-theatre mob. Come here for a coffee and the view, not the food or the service.

VELRYBA (THE WHALE)

Opatovická 24. Daily 11am–midnight. MAP P.97, POCKET MAP G14

Classic student café – smoky, loud and serving cheap Czech food (lots of vegetarian options) and a ridiculously wide range of malt whiskies.

Restaurants

CICALA

Žitná 43 ☎ 222 210 375. Mon–Sat 11.30am–10.30pm. MAP P.97, POCKET MAP H15

Very good family-run Italian basement restaurant specializing (mid-week) in fresh seafood (from 300Kč). There's also a wide range of pasta (180–240Kč) and an appetizing antipasto selection.

ČINSKÁ RESTAURACE PO SEČUÁNSKU

Národní 25 ☎ 224 085 331. Daily 10am–11pm. MAP P.97, POCKET MAP G13

Hidden inside the Palác Metro *pasáž*, this is an inexpensive, unpretentious Sichuan restaurant dishing up steaming plates of authentic Chinese food for 150–250Kč.

DYNAMO

Pštrossova 29 ☎ 224 932 020. Daily 11.30am–midnight. MAP P.97, POCKET MAP F14

Fashionable little spot with eye-catching retro-1960s designer decor, inexpensive vegetarian and pasta dishes (125–150Kč) and steaks and Czech dishes for around 200Kč.

LEMON LEAF

Myslíkova 14 ☎ 224 919 056. Mon–Thurs 11am–11pm, Fri 11am–12.30am, Sat 12.30pm–12.30am, Sun 12.30pm–11pm. MAP P.97, POCKET MAP F15

Clean and bright Thai restaurant, serving up spicy meat and fish curries (170–250Kč). The weekday lunchtime menus (100–130Kč) are very popular as is the all-you-can-eat weekend brunch (240Kč).

PIZZERIA KMOTRA (GODMOTHER)

V jirchářích 12 ☎ 224 934 100. Daily 11am–midnight. MAP P.97, POCKET MAP F14

This inexpensive, brick-vaulted basement pizza place is popular, and justifiably so – if possible, book a table in advance. Pizzas 110–160Kč.

POSEZENÍ U ČIRINY

Navrátilova 6 ☎ 222 231 709. Mon–Sat 11am–11pm. MAP P.97, POCKET MAP G14

A little family-run place, with

GLOBE

only a handful of tables inside, leather benches in cosy wooden alcoves, and a summer terrace. Classic Slovak home cooking for around 200Kč, including national dish *Bryndzové halusky*, similar to gnocchi with sheep's cheese.

STŘELECKÝ OSTROV

Střelecký ostrov ☎ 603 775 662. Daily 11am–11pm. MAP P.97, POCKET MAP E14

The kitchen here serves up classic Czech cuisine (mains from around 300Kč), but it's the location – on an island in the Vltava, with an outdoor terrace overlooking the National Theatre – that pulls in the punters.

ŽOFÍN GARDEN

Slovanský ostrov ☎ 774 774 774. Mon–Sat 11am–11pm. MAP P.97, POCKET MAP E14

With a superb riverside location on the island nearest the National Theatre, *Žofín* serves up beautifully presented pizzas and pasta, barbecued fish, tiger prawns and rib-eye steak all for under 200Kč.

Pubs

BRANICKÝ SKLÍPEK

Vodičkova 26. Mon–Fri 9am–11pm, Sat & Sun 11am–11pm. MAP P.97, POCKET MAP H14

Convenient downtown pub (aka *U Purkmistra*) decked out like a pine furniture showroom serving typical Czech dishes and jugs of Prague's Braník beer. The rough-and-ready *Branická formanka* next door opens and closes earlier.

NOVOMĚSTSKÝ PIVOVAR

Vodičkova 20. Mon–Fri 10am–11.30pm, Sat 11.30am–11.30pm, Sun noon–10pm. MAP P.97, POCKET MAP G14

Microbrewery which serves its own misty home brew, plus Czech food, in a series of bright, sprawling modern beer halls.

PIVOVARKSÝ DŮM

Corner of Lipová/Ječná. Daily 11am–11.30pm. MAP P.97, POCKET MAP H15

Busy microbrewery dominated by big, shiny copper vats, serving gorgeous light, mixed and dark unfiltered beer (plus banana, coffee and wheat varieties), and standard Czech pub dishes.

PIVOVARKSÝ DŮM

POTREFENÁ HUSA (THE WOUNDED GOOSE)

Jiráskovo náměstí 1. Daily 11.30am–1am. MAP P.97, POCKET MAP F15

Staropramen's chain of smart pubs, serving decent pub food, have proved very popular; this one's in a cosy, brick-line cellar near the Fred & Ginger building (see p.102).

U FLEKŮ

Křemencova 11. Daily 9am–11pm. MAP P.97, POCKET MAP F14

Famous medieval brewery where the unique dark 13° beer, Flek, has been brewed since 1499. Seats over five hundred German tourists at a go, serves short measures (0.4l), charges extra for the music and still you might have to queue. The only reason to visit is to sample the beer, which you're best off doing during the day.

U HAVRANA (THE CROW)

Hálkova 6. Mon–Fri 5pm–5am, Sat 6pm–5am. MAP P.97 POCKET MAP J15

The chief virtue of this ordinary and surprisingly unseedy Czech pub is that it serves food and Velkopopovický kozel beer until the early hours of the morning.

U KRUHU (THE WHEEL)

Palackého 6. Mon–Fri 10am–10pm, Sat & Sun 2–10pm. MAP P.97, POCKET MAP H14

Proper Czech pub, serving Plzeň beers and Velkopovický kozel, with its own garden courtyard out front.

U PINKASŮ

Jungmannovo náměstí 16. Daily 9am–midnight. MAP P.97, POCKET MAP H13

Famous as the pub where Pilsner Urquell was first served in Prague, it still serves excellent unpasteurized beer and classic Czech pub food.

Clubs and venues

DIVADLO MINOR

Vodičkova 6 ☎ 222 231 351, Ⓦ www.minor.cz.
MAP P.97, POCKET MAP G14

The former state puppet theatre puts on children's shows most days, plus adult shows on occasional evenings, sometimes with English subtitles.

EVALD

Národní 28 ☎ 221 105 225, Ⓦ www.evald.cz.
MAP P.97, POCKET MAP G13

Prague's most centrally located arthouse cinema shows a discerning selection of new releases interspersed with plenty of classics.

LATERNA MAGIKA (MAGIC LANTERN)

Nová scéna, Národní 4 ☎ 224 931 482,
Ⓦ www.laterna.cz. MAP P.97, POCKET MAP F14

The National Theatre's Nová scéna, one of the city's most modern and versatile stages, is the main base for Laterna magika, founders of multimedia and "black light" theatre way back in 1958. Their slick productions continue effortlessly to pull in crowds of curious tourists.

MAT STUDIO

Karlovo náměstí 19, entrance on Odborů
☎ 224 915 765, Ⓦ www.mat.cz. MAP P.97,
POCKET MAP G15

Tiny café and cinema popular with the film crowd, with an eclectic programme of shorts, documentaries and Czech films with English subtitles.

N11

Národní 11 ☎ 222 075 705, Ⓦ www.n11.cz.
Tues–Sun. MAP P.97, POCKET MAP F13

Medium-sized club with several bars, an average restaurant, a decent sound system and DJs who play a popular mix of pop, rock and reggae.

NATIONAL THEATRE (NÁRODNÍ DIVADLO)

Národní 2 ☎ 224 901 487, Ⓦ www
.narodni-divadlo.cz. MAP P.97, POCKET MAP F14

Prague's National Theatre is the living embodiment of the Czech national revival movement and worth visiting for the decor alone. Czech plays form the bedrock of the repertoire, but ballet and opera feature too, the latter with English subtitles.

THE NATIONAL THEATRE

REDUTA

Národní 20 ☎ 224 933 487, Ⓦ www
.redutajazzclub.cz. Daily from 9.30pm.
MAP P.97, POCKET MAP G13

Prague's best-known jazz club – Bill Clinton played his sax here in front of Havel – attracts a touristy crowd, but also some decent acts.

ROCK CAFÉ

Národní 20. Mon–Fri 10am–3am, Sat 5pm–3am, Sun 6pm–1am. MAP P.97
POCKET MAP G13

Not to be confused with the *Hard Rock Café*, this place is a stalwart of the live music scene; the basement stage showcases mostly new Czech bands. Admission 100–150Kč.

Vyšehrad, Vinohrady and Žižkov

The fortress of Vyšehrad makes for a perfect afternoon escape away from the human congestion of the city centre: its cemetery shelters the remains of Bohemia's artistic elite; the ramparts afford superb views over the river; and below the fortress there are several interesting examples of Czech Cubist architecture. Vinohrady, to the east, is a late nineteenth-century residential suburb, dominated by long streets of grandiose apartment blocks, with one or two specific sights to guide your wandering. By contrast, Žižkov, further north, is a grittier working-class district, whose shabby, rundown streets contain some of the city's best pubs and clubs.

CUBIST VILLAS

MAP OPPOSITE, POCKET MAP D8

Even if you harbour only a passing interest in modern architecture, it's worth seeking out the cluster of **Cubist villas** below the fortress in Vyšehrad. The most impressive example is the apartment block at **Neklanova 30**, begun in 1913, which brilliantly exploits its angular location. Further along Neklanova at no. 2, there's another Cubist facade, and around the corner is the most ambitious of the lot, the **Kovařovicova vila**, which uses prism shapes and angular lines to produce the sharp geometric contrasts of light and dark shadows characteristic of Cubist painting.

CUBIST VILLA

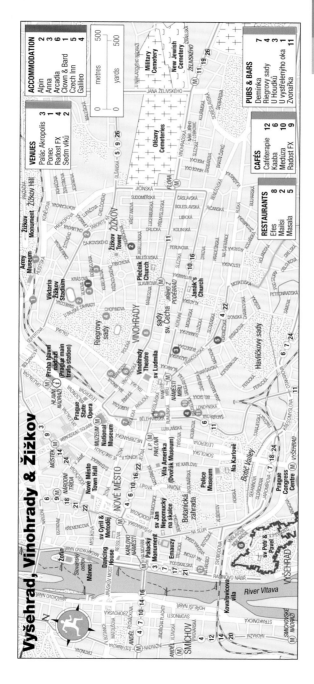

Vyšehrad, Vinohrady & Žižkov

ACCOMMODATION

Alpin	2
Anna	3
Arcadia	6
Clown & Bard	1
Czech Inn	5
Galileo	4

VENUES

Palác Akropolis	3
Ponec	1
Radost FX	4
Sedm vlků	2

PUBS & BARS

Deminka	7
Riegrovy sady	4
U Houdků	3
U vystřeleného oka	1
Zvonařka	11

CAFÉS

Caféterapie	12
Kaaba	6
Medúza	10
Radost FX	9

RESTAURANTS

Efes	8
Mailsi	2
Masala	5

VYŠEHRAD

V pevnosti 5b ⓦ www.praha-vysehrad.cz.
Open 24hr. Free. MAP P.109, POCKET MAP D9

The rocky red-brick fortress of **Vyšehrad** – literally "High Castle" – has more myths attached to it than any other place in Bohemia. According to Czech legend, this is the place where the Slav tribes first settled in Prague and where the "wise and tireless chieftain" Krok built a castle, whence his youngest daughter Libuše went on to found Praha itself. Alas, the archeological evidence doesn't really bear this claim out. What you see now are the remains of a fortified barracks built by the Habsburgs and then turned into a public park.

You can explore the fortress's northern entrance, or **Cihelná brána** (daily: April–Oct 9.30am–6pm; Nov–March 9.30am–5pm; 10Kč), and the adjacent **dungeons** or *kasematy* (same hours; 30Kč). After a short guided tour of a section of the underground passageways underneath the ramparts, you enter a vast storage hall, which shelters several of the original statues from the Charles Bridge, and, when the lights are switched

Getting to Vyšehrad

To reach Vyšehrad, take tram #3, #7, #17 or #21 to Výtoň, and either wind your way up Vratislavova to the Cihelná brána or take the steep stairway from Rašínovo nábřeží that leads up through the trees. Alternatively, from Vyšehrad metro station, walk west past the ugly Prague Congress Centre, and enter via V pevnosti, where there's an information centre (daily: April–Oct 9.30am–6pm; Nov–March 9.30am–5pm).

off, reveals a camera obscura image of a tree.

Over in the southwestern corner of the fortress, in the **Gothic cellar** (same hours; 30Kč), there's also a permanent exhibition on the history of Vyšehrad. The rock's big moment in Czech history was in the eleventh century when Přemysl Vratislav II – the first Bohemian ruler to bear the title "king" – built a royal palace here to get away from his younger brother who was lording it in the Hrad. Within half a century the royals had moved back to Hradčany, into a new palace, and from then on Vyšehrad began to lose its political significance.

CHURCH OF SV PETR AND PAVEL

K rotundě 10. Tues–Thurs & Sat 9am–noon & 1–5pm, Fri 9am–noon, Sun 10am–noon & 1–5pm. 30Kč. MAP P.109, POCKET MAP D9

The twin open-work spires of this blackened sandstone church, rebuilt in the 1880s in neo-Gothic style on the site of an eleventh-century basilica, are now the fortress's most familiar landmark. Inside, you can admire the church's **Art Nouveau murals** which cover every available surface.

DOORS OF THE CHURCH OF SV PETR AND PAVEL

VYŠEHRAD CEMETERY (VYŠEHRADSKÝ HŘBITOV)

Ⓦ www.slavin.cz. Daily: March, April & Oct 8am–6pm; May–Sept 8am–7pm; Nov–Feb 8am–5pm. Free. MAP P.109, POCKET MAP D9

Most Czechs come to Vyšehrad to pay a visit to the **cemetery**. It's a measure of the part that artists and intellectuals played in the foundation of the nation, and the regard in which they are still held, that the most prestigious graveyard in the city is given over to them: no soldiers, no politicians – not even the Communists managed to muscle their way in here (except on artistic merit). Sheltered from the wind by its high walls, lined on two sides by delicate arcades, it's a tiny cemetery filled with well-kept graves, many of them designed by the country's leading sculptors.

To the uninitiated only a handful of figures are well known, but for the Czechs the place is alive with great names (there's a useful plan of the most notable graves at the entrance nearest the church). Ladislav Šaloun's grave for **Dvořák**, situated under the arches, is one of the more showy ones, with a mosaic inscription, studded with gold stones, glistening behind wrought-iron railings. **Smetana**, who died twenty years earlier, is buried in comparatively modest surroundings near the **Slavín monument**, the cemetery's focal point, which is the communal resting place of more than fifty Czech artists, including the painter Alfons Mucha and the opera singer Ema Destinová. The grave of the Romantic poet Karel Hynek Mácha was the assembly point for the demonstration on November 17, 1989, which triggered the Velvet Revolution. This was organized to commemorate the fiftieth anniversary of the Nazi closure of Czech higher education institutions. A 50,000-strong crowd gathered here and attempted to march to Wenceslas Square, getting as far as Národní before being beaten back (see p.98).

VILA AMERIKA

POLICE MUSEUM

Ke Karlovu 1, metro Vyšehrad. Tues–Sun
10am–5pm. 30Kč. MAP P.109, POCKET MAP E8

The former Augustinian
monastery of Karlov houses
the **Police Museum**, which
concentrates on road and
traffic offences, and the force's
latest challenges: forgery,
drugs and murder. There's a
whole section on the old Iron
Curtain and espionage, but not
a huge amount of information
in English. If you've got kids,
however, they might enjoy
driving round the mini-road
layout on one of the museum
trikes.

NA KARLOVĚ CHURCH

Ke Karlovu, metro Vyšehrad. No set hours.
Free. MAP P.109, POCKET MAP E8

Founded by Emperor Charles
IV and designed in imitation of
Charlemagne's tomb in Aachen,
this octagonal church is quite
unlike any other in Prague.
If it's open, you should take a
look at the dark interior, which
was remodelled in the sixteenth
century by Bonifaz Wohlmut.
The stellar vault has no

central supporting pillars – a
remarkable feat of engineering
for its time, and one which
gave rise to numerous legends
about the architect being in
league with the devil.

VILA AMERIKA (DVOŘÁK MUSEUM)

Ke Karlovu 20, metro I. P. Pavlova. April–Sept
Tues, Wed & Fri–Sun 10am–1.30pm & 2–5pm,
Thurs 11am–3.30pm & 4–7pm; Oct–March
Tues–Sun 10am–1.30pm & 2–5pm. 50Kč.
MAP P.109, POCKET MAP E7

The russet-coloured **Vila
Amerika** was originally named
after the local pub, but is now
a museum devoted to **Antonín
Dvořák** (1841–1904), the most
famous of all Czech composers,
who lived for a time on nearby
Zitná. Even if you've no interest
in Dvořák, the villa itself is
a delight, built as a Baroque
summer house from around
1720. The tasteful period
rooms, with the composer's
music wafting in and out,
and the tiny garden dotted
with Baroque sculptures,
compensate for what the
display cabinets may lack.

NÁMĚSTÍ MÍRU

MAP P.109, POCKET MAP F7

If Vinohrady has a centre, it's the leafy square of **náměstí Míru**, a good introduction to this neighbourhood. The most flamboyant building here is the **Vinohrady Theatre** (Divadlo na Vinohradech), built in 1907, with both Art Nouveau and neo-Baroque elements. At the centre of the square stands the brick basilica of **sv Ludmila**, designed in the late 1880s in a severe neo-Gothic style, though the interior has the odd flourish of Art Nouveau. In front a statue commemorates the **Čapek brothers**, writer Karel and painter Josef, local residents who together symbolized the golden era of the interwar republic. Karel died of pneumonia in 1938 while Josef perished in Belsen seven years later.

PLEČNIK CHURCH

Náměstí Jiřího z Poděbrad, metro Jiřího z Poděbrad. No set hours. Free. MAP P.109, POCKET MAP G7

Prague's most celebrated modern church is **Nejsvětějšího Srdce Páně** (Most Sacred Heart of Our Lord), built in 1928 by the Slovene architect **Josip Plečnik**. It's a marvellously eclectic work, employing a sophisticated potpourri of architectural styles: a Neoclassical pediment and a great slab of a clock tower with a giant transparent face in imitation of a Gothic rose window, as well as the bricks and mortar of contemporary constructivism. Plečnik also had a sharp eye for detail; look out for the little gold crosses inset into the brickwork like stars, inside and out, and the celestial orbs of light suspended above the congregation.

ŽIŽKOV TOWER (TELEVIZNÍ VĚŽ)

Mahlerovy sady 1, metro Jiřího z Poděbrad. Ⓦ www.tower.cz. Daily 10am–11.30pm. 150Kč. MAP P.109, POCKET MAP G6

At 216m in height, the Žižkov **TV tower** is the tallest building in Prague. Close up, it's an intimidating futuristic piece of architecture, made all the more disturbing thanks to the giant babies crawling up the sides, courtesy of artist **David Černý**. Begun in the 1970s in a desperate bid to jam West German television transmissions, the tower became fully operational only in the 1990s. In the course of its construction, however, the Communists saw fit to demolish part of a nearby **Jewish cemetery** that had served the community between 1787 and 1891; a small section survives to the northwest of the tower. From the **fifth-floor café** or the **viewing platform** on the eighth floor, you can enjoy a spectacular view across Prague.

ŽIŽKOV TV TOWER

OLŠANY CEMETERIES (OLŠANY HŘBITOVY)

Vinohradská, metro Flora. Daily dawn–dusk. Free. MAP P.109, POCKET MAP H6–J6

The vast Olšany cemeteries were originally created for the victims of the great plague epidemic of 1680. The perimeter walls are lined with glass cabinets, stacked like shoe-boxes, containing funereal urns and mementoes, while the graves themselves are a mixed bag of artistic achievements, reflecting the funereal fashions of the day as much as the character of the deceased. The cemeteries are divided into districts and crisscrossed with cobbled streets; at each gate there's a map and an aged janitor ready to point you in the right direction.

The cemeteries' two most famous incumbents are an ill-fitting couple: **Klement Gottwald**, the country's first Communist president, whose remains were removed from the mausoleum on Žižkov hill after 1989 and reinterred here; and **Jan Palach**, the philosophy student who set light to himself in January 1969 in protest at the Soviet occupation. More than 750,000 people attended Palach's funeral, and in an attempt to put a stop to the annual vigils at his graveside, the secret police removed his body and reburied him in his home town outside Prague. In 1990, Palach's body was returned to Olšany; you'll find it just to the east of the main entrance.

NEW JEWISH CEMETERY (NOVÝ ŽIDOVSKÝ HŘBITOV)

Izraelská 1, metro Želivského. April–Sept Mon–Thurs & Sun 9am–4.30pm, Fri 9am–2.30pm; Oct–March Mon–Thurs & Sun 9am–3.30pm, Fri 9am–1.30pm. 50Kč. MAP P.109, POCKET MAP K6

Founded in the 1890s, the **New Jewish Cemetery** was designed to last for a century, with room for 100,000 graves. It's a melancholy spot, particularly so in the east of the cemetery, where large empty allotments wait in vain to be filled by the generation that perished in the Holocaust. Most people come here to visit **Franz Kafka's grave**, 400m east along the south wall and signposted from the entrance. He is buried, along with his mother and father (both of whom outlived him), beneath a plain headstone; the plaque below commemorates his three sisters who died in the camps.

GRAVESTONE AT OLŠANY

THE ARMY MUSEUM

ŽIŽKOV HILL

U památníku, bus #133 or #207 from metro Florenc. MAP P.109; POCKET MAP G5–H5

Žižkov Hill is the thin green wedge of land that separates Žižkov from Karlín, the grid-plan industrial district to the north. From its westernmost point, which juts out almost to the edge of Nové Město, is the definitive panoramic view over the city centre. It was here, on July 14, 1420, that the Hussites enjoyed their first and finest victory at the **Battle of Vítkov**, under the inspired leadership of the one-eyed general, Jan Žižka (hence the name of the district). Ludicrously outnumbered by more than ten to one, Žižka and his fanatically motivated troops thoroughly trounced the Bohemian King (and Holy Roman Emperor Sigismund) and his papal forces.

Despite its totalitarian aesthetics, the giant concrete **Žižkov monument**, which graces the crest of the hill, was actually built between the wars as a memorial to the Czechoslovak Legion who fought against the Habsburgs in the World War I – the gargantuan statue of the mace-wielding Žižka, which fronts the monument, is reputedly the world's largest equestrian statue. The building was later used by the Nazis as an arsenal, and eventually became a Communist mausoleum. In 1990, the Communists were cremated and quietly reinterred in Olšany. The monument now houses a fascinating **museum** (Wed–Sun 10am–6pm; 110Kč) on the country's twentieth-century history, a Communist monument to the fallen of World War II, and a café on top, with great views over Prague's suburbs.

ARMY MUSEUM (ARMÁDNÍ MUZEUM)

U památníku 2, bus #133 or #207 from metro Florenc ⓦ www.vhu.cz. Tues–Sun 10am–6pm. Free. MAP P.109; POCKET MAP G5

Guarded by a handful of unmanned tanks, howitzers and armoured vehicles, the **Army Museum** has a permanent exhibition covering the country's military history from 1914 to 1945. A fairly evenly balanced account of both world wars includes coverage of controversial subjects such as the exploits of the Czechoslovak Legion, the Heydrich assassination and the 1945 Prague Uprising.

Cafés

CAFÉTERAPIE

Na hrobci 3. Mon–Fri 10am–10pm, Sat & Sun noon–10pm. MAP P.109, POCKET MAP D8

Small, simply furnished café that serves up nice healthy Mediterranean-influenced salads, sandwiches, toasties and a few hot dishes.

KAABA

Mánesova 20. Mon–Fri 8am–10pm, Sat 9am–10pm, Sun 10am–10pm. MAP P.109, POCKET MAP K14

This stylish ice-cream parlour of a café attracts a young trendy crowd with its mismatched 1950s repro chairs and tables. Serves breakfast, sandwiches, salads, soup and toasties.

MEDÚZA

Belgická 17. Mon–Fri 10am–1am, Sat & Sun noon–1am. MAP P.109 POCKET MAP F7.

A deliberately faded, inexpensive café, which displays art and photography by local artists and serves breakfast and *palačinky* all day. Free wi-fi.

RADOST FX CAFÉ

Bělehradská 120. Daily 11am–midnight. MAP P.109, POCKET MAP J15

The veggie dishes at this expat favourite are filling and all under 200Kč, the decor is decadent and there's a dance soundtrack (with live DJs at the weekend). However, it can be a disappointing culinary experience. Free wi-fi.

Restaurants

EFES

Vinohradská 63 ☏ 222 250 015. Mon–Sat 11.30am–11pm. MAP P.109, POCKET MAP F7

Honest Turkish grilled meats for under 200Kč with all the trimmings, *cacik*, hummus and fresh bread – veggie dishes like *ayvar*, or bulgar wheat and aubergine, are also available.

MAILSI

Lipanská 1 ☏ 222 717 783. Daily noon–3pm & 6pm–midnight. MAP P.109, POCKET MAP G6

Prague's only Pakistani restaurant is a friendly, unpretentious Punjabi place that's great for a comfort curry for around 300Kč, as hot as you can handle. The decor includes a wall of built-in aquariums.

MASALA

Mánesova 13 ☏ 773 555 652. Mon–Fri 11.30am–10.30pm, Sat & Sun 12.30–10.30pm. MAP P.109, POCKET MAP K14

This North Indian restaurant is justifiably popular with the local expats. The Tandoori kebabs and kormas (160–260Kč) are authentically spicy and the naan bread is homemade and the Jain brothers who run it are genuinely friendly.

Pubs and bars

DEMÍNKA

Škrétova 1. Daily 11am–11pm. MAP P.109, POCKET MAP J15

With much of its original grandiose 1880s decor intact – it is Prague's oldest café – *Demínka* is now run as a pub

RADOST FX CAFÉ

by Pilsner Urquell, who serve their excellent unpasteurized beer and classic Bohemian cuisine.

RIEGROVY SADY

Riegrovy sady. Daily 11am–11pm. MAP P.109, POCKET MAP G6

A real slice of local life, a neighbourhood park café-pub whose beer terrace is perennially popular, especially for big TV sports events.

U HOUDKŮ

Bořivojova 110. Daily 11am–11pm. MAP P.109, POCKET MAP G6

Friendly local pub in the heart of Žižkov with a beer garden, Eggenberg and Budvar on tap and cheap Czech food.

U VYSTŘELENÝHO OKA (THE SHOT-OUT EYE)

U božích bojovníků 3. Mon–Sat 4.30pm–1am. MAP P.109, POCKET MAP G5

Big, loud, smoky, heavy-drinking pub with unusually good (occasionally live) indie rock and lashings of Měšťan beer, plus absinthe chasers.

ZVONAŘKA (THE BELL)

Šafaříkova 1. Daily 11am–midnight. MAP P.109, POCKET MAP F8

The smart modern pub has a summer terrace with great views over the Nuselské schody and Botič valley.

Clubs and venues

PALÁC AKROPOLIS

Kubelíkova 27 ☎ 296 330 911, ⓦ www .palacakropolis.cz. Mon–Thurs 11am–12.30am, Fri 11am–1.30am, Sat & Sun 3pm–12.30am. MAP P.109, POCKET MAP G6

This old Art Deco theatre is Žižkov's most popular club

venue – it's also a great place to just have a drink or a bite to eat, as well as checking out the DJ nights or the live gigs. Cover charge 100Kč and upwards for events.

PONEC

Husitská 24a ☎ 222 721 531, ⓦ www .divadloponec.cz. MAP P.109, POCKET MAP G5

Former cinema, now an innovative dance venue and centre for the annual Tanec Praha dance festival in June.

RADOST FX

Bělehradská 120 ☎ 224 254 776, ⓦ www .radostfx.cz. Thurs–Sat 10pm–4am. MAP P.109, POCKET MAP J15

This spacious, comfortable club is the longest-running all-round dance venue in Prague, with house and techno keeping the expats happy. Up to 250Kč entrance depending on the night.

SEDM VLKŮ (SEVEN WOLVES)

Vlkova 33 ☎ 222 711 725, ⓦ www.sedmvlku .cz. Mon–Sat 5pm–3am. MAP P.109, POCKET MAP G6

Club-bar with a penchant for reggae, hard house, techno and drum'n'bass whose resident DJs make the most of the impressive sound system.

RADOST FX

Holešovice

Tucked into a huge U-bend in the River Vltava, the late nineteenth-century suburb of Holešovice boasts two huge splodges of green: Letná, overlooking the city centre, and, to the north, Stromovka, the city's largest public park, bordering the Výstaviště funfair and trade fair grounds. A stroll through the park gives you access to the Baroque chateau of Troja and the city's leafy zoo. However, the single most important sight in Holešovice is the Veletržní Palace, which houses the city's main museum of modern art. Only a trickle of tourists make it out here, but it's worth the effort, if only to remind yourself that Prague doesn't begin and end at the Charles Bridge.

LETNÁ

MAP OPPOSITE, POCKET MAP D4

A high plateau hovering above the city, the flat green expanse of the **Letná** plain has long been the traditional assembly point for invading and besieging armies. Under the Communists, it was used primarily for the annual May Day parades, during which thousands trudged past the Sparta Prague stadium, where the Communist leaders would salute from their giant red podium. It once boasted the largest **Stalin monument** in the world: a 30-metre-high granite sculpture portraying a procession of Czechs and Russians being led to Communism by the Pied Piper figure of Stalin, but popularly dubbed *tlačenice* (the crush) because of its resemblance to a Communist-era bread queue. The monument was unveiled on May 1, 1955, but within a year Khrushchev had denounced Stalin, and the monument was blown up in 1962. On the site of the Stalin statue, overlooking the Vltava, stands David Černý's symbolic giant red **metronome** (which is lit up at night).

THE VIEW FROM LETNÁ

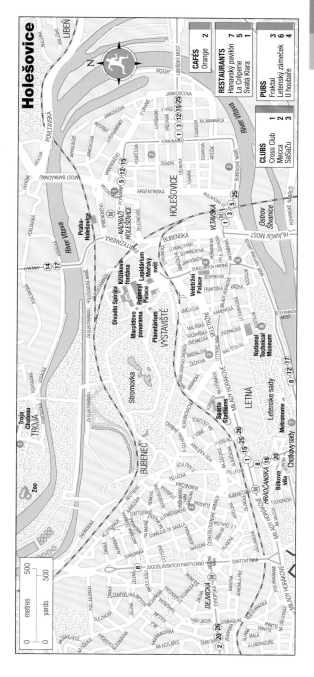

Holešovice

CAFÉS

Orange	2

RESTAURANTS

Hanavský pavilón	7
La Crêperie	5
Svatá Klara	1

PUBS

Fraktal	3
Letenský zámeček	6
U houbaře	4

CLUBS

Cross Club	1
Mecca	2
SaSaZu	3

BÍLKOVA VILA

Mieckiewiczova 1 🔵 www.villabilekcentre
.cz. Sat & Sun 10am–5pm. 50Kč. MAP P.119.
POCKET MAP C4

The **Bílkova vila** honours
one of the most original of all
Czech sculptors, **František
Bílek** (1872–1941). Built in
1911 to the artist's own design,
the house was intended as
both a "cathedral of art" and
the family home. Inside,
Bílek's extravagant religious
sculptures line the walls of
his "workshop and temple".
In addition to his sculptural
and relief work in wood and
stone, often wildly expressive
and spiritually tortured, there
are also ceramics, graphics and
a few mementoes of Bílek's
life. His living quarters have
also been restored and have
much of the original wooden
furniture, designed and carved
by Bílek himself, still in place.
Check out the dressing table
for his wife, shaped like some
giant church lectern, and the
wardrobe decorated with a
border of hearts, a penis, a
nose, an ear and an eye plus
the sun, stars and moon.

CHOTKOVY SADY

MAP P.119, POCKET MAP C4

Prague's first public park, the
Chotkovy sady, was founded
in 1833 by the ecologically
minded city governor, Count
Chotek. The atmosphere
here is relaxed and you can
happily stretch out on the
grass and soak up the sun, or
head for the south wall, for an
unrivalled view of the bridges
and islands of the Vltava. At
the centre of the park there's
a bizarre, melodramatic
grotto-like memorial to the
nineteenth-century Romantic
poet **Julius Zeyer**, an elaborate
monument from which
life-sized characters from
Zeyer's works, carved in white
marble, emerge from the
blackened rocks.

NATIONAL TECHNICAL MUSEUM (NÁRODNÍ TECHNICKÉ MUZEUM)

Kostelní 42 🔵 www.ntm.cz. Closed until 2011.
MAP P.119, POCKET MAP E4

Despite its dull name, this
museum is surprisingly
interesting, with a showpiece
hangar-like main hall
containing an impressive
gallery of motorbikes, Czech
and foreign, and a wonderful
collection of old planes,
trains and automobiles from
Czechoslovakia's industrial
heyday between the wars when
the country's Škoda cars and
Tatra soft-top stretch limos
were really something to

brag about. The oldest car in the collection is Laurin and Klement's 1898 Präsident, more of a motorized carriage than a car; the museum also boasts the oldest Bugatti in the world. Other displays trace the development of early photography, and there's also a collection of some of Kepler and Tycho Brahe's astrological instruments.

VELETRŽNÍ PALACE (TRADE FAIR PALACE)

Dukelských hrdinů 45 ⓦ www.ngprague.cz. Tues–Sun 10am–6pm. 200Kč (100Kč after 4pm). MAP P.119, POCKET MAP E3

The **Veletržní Palace** gets nothing like the number of visitors it should. For not only does the building house the city's best twentieth-century Czech and international art collection, it is also an architectural sight in itself. Built in 1928, the palace is Prague's ultimate functionalist masterpiece, not so much from the outside, but inside, where its gleaming white vastness is suitably awesome.

The gallery is both big and bewildering, and virtually impossible to view in its entirety in a single visit. Special exhibitions occupy the ground, first and fifth floors, while the permanent collection occupies the second, third and fourth floors. The popular **French art collection** includes works by Rodin, Renoir, Van Gogh, Matisse and Picasso. The rest of the "foreign art" (as it's called) includes works by Surrealist Miró, a couple of Henry Moore sculptures and a perforated Lucio Fontana canvas, plus a few canvases by Klimt, Kokoschka, Schiele and Munch, whose influence on early twentieth-century Czech art was considerable.

The **Czech art** section starts with Impressionists Preisler and Slavíček, Cubists Čapek, Gutfreund, Filla and Kubišta, and a whole series of works by **František Kupka**, by far the most important Czech painter of the last century, who secured his place in the history of art by being (possibly) the first artist in the western world to exhibit abstract paintings.

Elsewhere, there's an excellent **Socialist Realism** section, heralded by Karel Pokorný's monumental *Fraternisation* sculpture, in which a Czechoslovak soldier is engaging in a "kiss of death" with a Soviet comrade. Performance art (umění akce) – big in the 1960s, even in Communist Czechoslovakia – has its own section, which is undoubtedly worth a giggle. The gallery also owns several works by Jiří Kolář – pronounced "collage" – who, coincidentally, specializes in collages of random words and reproductions of other people's paintings.

VELETRŽNÍ PALACE

VÝSTAVIŠTĚ (EXHIBITION GROUNDS)

Dukelských hrdinů Ⓦ www.incheba.cz. Tues–Fri 2–9pm, Sat & Sun 10am–9pm. 20Kč or free. MAP P.119, POCKET MAP E2

Since the 1891 Prague Exhibition, **Výstaviště** has served as the city's main trade fair arena and funfair. At the centre of the complex is the flamboyant stained-glass and wrought-iron **Průmysl Palace**, scene of Communist Party rubber-stamp congresses. Several modern structures were built for the 1991 Prague Exhibition, including a circular theatre, **Divadlo Spirála**.

The grounds are busiest at the weekend, particularly in summer, when hordes of Prague families descend on the place to wolf down hot dogs and drink beer. Apart from the annual trade fairs and special exhibitions, there are a few permanent attractions: the city's **Planetárium** (times vary; 50–150Kč; Ⓦ www .planetarium.cz), which has static displays and shows films; the **Maroldovo panorama** (April–Oct Tues–Fri 1–5pm, Sat & Sun 10am–5pm; 25Kč), a giant diorama of the 1434 Battle of Lipany; and **Mořský svět** (daily 10am–7pm; 240Kč; Ⓦ www.morsky-svet.cz), an aquarium full of countless colourful tropical fish, a few rays and some sea turtles. In the long summer evenings, there's also an open-air cinema (*letní kino*), and hourly evening performances (200Kč) by the **Křižík Fountain**, dancing fountains devised for the 1891 Exhibition by the Czech inventor František Křižík. Call ☏ 220 103 280 or visit Ⓦ www .krizikovafontana.cz for details of performances.

LAPIDÁRIUM

U Výstaviště Ⓦ www.nm.cz. Tues–Sun noon–6pm. 40Kč. MAP P.119, POCKET MAP E2

Official depository for the city's sculptures which are under threat either from demolition or from the weather, the **Lapidárium** houses a much overlooked collection, ranging from the eleventh to the nineteenth centuries. Some of the statues saved from the perils of Prague's polluted atmosphere, such as the bronze equestrian statue of St George, will be familiar if you've visited Prague Castle; others, such as the figures from the towers of the Charles Bridge, are more difficult to inspect closely in their original sites. Many of the original statues from the bridge can be seen here, as well as the ones that were fished out of the Vltava after the flood of 1890.

PRŮMYSL PALACE, VÝSTAVIŠTĚ

Getting to Troja and the Zoo

To reach Troja and the Zoo you can either **walk** from Výstaviště, catch **bus** #112, which runs frequently from metro Nádraží Holešovice, or take a **boat** (April & Oct Sat & Sun only; May–Sept daily; 140Kč; ⓦ www.paroplavba.cz) from the PPS landing place on Rašínovo nábřeží, metro Karlovo náměstí.

One outstanding sight is what remains of the **Krocín fountain**, a highly ornate Renaissance work in red marble, which used to grace Staroměstské náměstí (see p.66). Several pompous imperial monuments that were bundled into storage after the demise of the Habsburgs in 1918 round off the museum's collection. By far the most impressive is the bronze statue of Marshal Radecký, scourge of the 1848 revolution, carried aloft on a shield by eight Habsburg soldiers.

STROMOVKA

MAP P.119, POCKET MAP D2

Originally laid out as hunting grounds for the noble occupants of the Castle, **Stromovka** is now Prague's largest and leafiest public park. If you're heading north for Troja and the city zoo, a stroll through the park is by far the most pleasant approach. If you want to explore a little more of the park, head west sticking to the park's southern border and you'll eventually come to a neo-Gothic former royal hunting chateau, which served as the seat of the Governor of Bohemia until 1918.

TROJA CHATEAU (TROJSKÝ ZÁMEK)

U trojského zámku 1. April–Oct Tues–Thurs, Sat & Sun 10am–6pm, Fri 1–6pm. 120Kč. MAP P.119, POCKET MAP C1

The **Troja** chateau was designed by Jean-Baptiste Mathey for the powerful Šternberg family towards the end of the seventeenth century. The best features of the rusty-red Baroque facade are the monumental balustrades, where blackened figures of giants and titans battle it out. The star exhibits of the interior are the gushing frescoes depicting the victories of the Habsburg Emperor Leopold I (who reigned from 1657 to 1705) over the Turks, which cover every inch of the walls and ceilings of the grand hall. You also get to wander through the chateau's pristine, trend-setting, French-style formal gardens, the first of their kind in Bohemia.

TROJA CHATEAU

PRAGUE ZOO
(ZOOLOGICKÁ ZAHRADA)

U trojského zámku 3 ⓦ www.zoopraha.cz.
Daily: March 9am–5pm; April, May, Sept &
Oct 9am–6pm; June–Aug 9am–7pm; Nov–Feb
9am–4pm. 150Kč. MAP P.119, POCKET MAP C1

Founded in 1931 on the site
of one of Troja's numerous
hillside vineyards, Prague's **zoo**
has had a lot of money poured
into it and now has some very
imaginative enclosures. All
the usual animals are on show
here – including elephants,
hippos, giraffes, zebras, big
cats and bears – and kids, at
least, will enjoy themselves.
A bonus in the summer is the
fact you can take a **chairlift**
(*lanová dráha*) from the duck
pond over the enclosures to
the top of the hill, where the
prize exhibits – a rare breed
of miniature horse known as
Przewalski – hang out. Other
highlights include the red
pandas, the giant tortoises, the
Komodo dragons and the bats
that actually fly past your face
in the Twilight Zone.

BOTANIC GARDENS
(BOTANICKÁ ZAHRADA)

Nádvorní 134 ⓦ www.botanicka.cz. Daily:
March & Oct 9am–5pm; April 9am–6pm;
May–Sept 9am–7pm; Nov–Feb 9am–4pm.
120Kč. OFF MAP

Another reason for coming
out to Troja is to visit the city's
botanic gardens, hidden in
the woods to the north of the
chateau. The botanic gardens
feature a vineyard, a Japanese
garden, several glasshouses
and great views over Prague.
Hidden in the woods a little
higher up the hill, there's also
a spectacular, curvaceous
greenhouse, **Fata Morgana**
(same hours but closed Mon),
with butterflies flitting
about amid the desert and
tropical plants.

HANAVSKÝ PAVILON

Café

ORANGE

Puškinovo náměstí 13. Mon–Sat 10am–11pm.
Sun 11am–3pm. MAP P.119, POCKET MAP B3
Trendy, brightly decorated café
with seats outside overlooking
a quiet square. It serves good
pasta dishes, bruschetta snacks,
fresh juices and ice cream.

Restaurants

HANAVSKÝ PAVILÓN

Letenské sady 173 ☎ 233 323 641. Tues–Sun
11am–1am. MAP P.119, POCKET MAP E10
Highly ornate wrought-iron
Art Nouveau pleasure
pavilion high above the
Vltava, with stunning views
from the terrace; Czech and
international mains 350–500Kč.

LA CRÊPERIE

Janovského 4 ☎ 220 878 040. Daily
9am–11pm. MAP P.119, POCKET MAP F3
Small, unpretentious,
inexpensive French-run
crêperie (with a kids' play area)
serving buckwheat *galette* and
sweet and savoury pancakes
(for around 120Kč), washed
down with Breton cider.

SVATÁ KLARA (SAINT CLARE)

U trojského zámku 35 ☎ 233 540 173. Daily
7pm–1am. MAP P.119, POCKET MAP C1
Formal restaurant, first opened
in 1679, in a romantic wine
cave setting near the zoo.
Specializes in fondues and
game dishes from 500Kč.

Pubs

FRAKTAL

Šmeralova 1. Daily 11am–midnight. MAP P.119,
POCKET MAP D3
Very popular expat cellar bar
with ad hoc funky furnishings,

exhibitions and occasional live
music, plus a beer garden and
kids' play area outside.

LETENSKÝ ZÁMEČEK

Letenské sady. Daily 11am–11.30pm.
MAP P.119, POCKET MAP E4
The beer garden, with its great
views down the Vltava, is
cheap and popular with the
locals (the restaurant has gone
upmarket and is less special).

U HOUBAŘE (THE MUSHROOM)

Dukelských hrdinů 30. Daily 11am–midnight.
MAP P.119, POCKET MAP E3
Comfortable local pub, directly
opposite the Veletržní Palace,
serving Pilsner Urquell and
inexpensive Czech pub food.

Clubs

CROSS CLUB

Plynární 23 ⓦ crossclub.cz. Daily noon–2am
or later. MAP P.119, POCKET MAP F2
Adhoc labyrinthine club on
several floors, decked out in
arty industrial decor, near
Nádraží Holešovice. The DJs on
each floor range from techno to
ambient. Entry free–120Kč.

MECCA

U Průhonu 3 ⓦ www.mecca.cz. Café/
restaurant: Mon–Thurs 10am–11pm, Fri & Sat
10am–6am; club: Mon–Thurs 8pm–2am, Fri &
Sat 8pm–6am. MAP P.119, POCKET MAP G2
Despite being out in the
grid-plan streets of Prague 7,
this coolly converted factory is
one of the most impressive and
popular clubs in Prague. Club
entry 100Kč and upwards.

SASAZU

Bubenské nábřeží 306 ☎ 284 097 444. ⓦ www
.sasazu.cz. MAP P.119, POCKET MAP D3
Prague's biggest, newest venue
is housed in Holešovice's vast
market complex and includes a
pan-Asian restaurant, a major
venue for live gigs and a club.

Accommodation

Compared to the price of beer, accommodation in Prague is very expensive. If you're looking for a double and can pay around 4000Kč (€150) a night then you'll find plenty of choice. At the other end of the scale, there are numerous hostels charging around 400Kč (€15) for a bed. However, there's a chronic shortage of decent, inexpensive to middle-range places. You can, however, get some very good deals – and undercut the often exorbitant rack rates – by booking online well in advance. Given that Prague can be pretty busy all year round, it's not a bad idea to book ahead in any case. All accommodation prices in this chapter are for the cheapest double room in high season; breakfast is usually included in the price, unless otherwise stated.

Hradčany

DOMUS HENRICI > Loretánská 11, tram #22 to Pohořelec ☎ 220 511 369, Ⓦ www.domus-henrici.cz. MAP P.40, POCKET MAP B11. Stylish, discreet hotel in a fabulous location, with just eight rooms/apartments, some with splendid views. Run in conjunction with *Domus Balthasar* on Mostecká, by the Charles Bridge. Free wi-fi. **Doubles from 4400Kč.**

QUESTENBERK > Úvoz 15, tram #22 from metro Malostranská to Pohořelec ☎ 220 407 600, Ⓦ www.questenberk .cz. MAP P.40, POCKET MAP A12. From the outside, this hotel looks like a Baroque chapel, but inside it's been totally modernized. Rooms are smart but plain, though the views from some are superb. **Doubles from 3000Kč.**

SAVOY > Keplerova 6, tram #22 from metro Malostranská to Pohořelec ☎ 224 302 430, Ⓦ www.savoyhotel.cz. MAP P.40, POCKET MAP A5. Super-luxury hotel on the western edge of Hradčany, concealed behind a pretty Art Nouveau facade and famous for its large marble bathrooms. This is one of Prague's finest, and as a result is popular with visiting celebs. **Doubles from 4500Kč.**

U KRÁLE KARLA (KING CHARLES) > Úvoz 4, tram #22 to Pohořelec ☎ 257 532 869, Ⓦ www.romantichotels.cz. MAP P.40, POCKET MAP B11. Possibly the most tastefully exquisite of all the small luxury hotels in the castle district, with beautiful antique furnishings and stained-glass windows. Situated at the top of Nerudova, it's a steep walk from the nearest tram stop, however. **Doubles from 4000Kč.**

U RAKA (THE CRAYFISH) > Černínská 10, tram #22 from metro Malostranská to Brusnice ☎ 220 511 100, Ⓦ www.romantikhotel-uraka.cz. MAP P.40, POCKET MAP A10. The perfect hideaway, six double rooms in a little half-timbered, eighteenth-century cottage in Nový Svět. No children under 12 or dogs and advance reservation a must. **Doubles from 3500Kč.**

U ZLATÉHO KONIČKA (GOLDEN HORSE) > Úvoz 8, tram #22 to Pohořelec ☎ 603 841 790, Ⓦ www .goldenhorse.cz. MAP P.40, POCKET MAP B11. Small, plain, clean, en-suite rooms at real bargain prices in a perfect location on the way up to the Hrad. Breakfast is served in the brick-vaulted cellar. **Doubles from 2350Kč.**

Malá Strana

ALCHYMIST GRAND HOTEL > Tržiště 19, tram #12, #20 or #22 to Malostranské náměstí ☏ 257 286 011, Ⓦ www.alchymisthotel .com. MAP P.48-49, POCKET MAP C12. Total decadent luxury abounds in this sixteenth-century palace, which has been tastefully converted into a secluded spa hotel, complete with Indonesian masseuses and an indoor pool. **Doubles from 9000Kč**.

ARIA > Tržiště 9, tram #12, #20 or #22 to Malostranské náměstí ☏ 225 334 111, Ⓦ www.ariahotel.net. MAP P.48-49, POCKET MAP C12. *Aria* is perhaps Prague's most popular boutique hotel, a superbly stylish, contemporary place complete with a stunning roof terrace and music-themed floors (and rooms) from jazz and rock to classical and opera. Breakfast is extra. **Doubles from 5000Kč**.

CASTLE STEPS > Nerudova 7, tram #12, #20 or #22 to Malostranské náměstí ☏ 257 216 337 (plus numerous international toll-free numbers, check their website), Ⓦ www.castlesteps.com. MAP P.48-49, POCKET MAP C11. This is without doubt Malá Strana's most amazing bargain: a variety of beautifully furnished rooms and apartments, some with unbelievable views, some with shared facilities, others with self-catering apartments, dotted around the vicinity. There's no reception as such, but an office where you check in (with free internet access). A fairly rudimentary vegan breakfast is served in a cellar (also with free internet) on Úvoz until 11am. **Doubles from 1500Kč**.

DIENTZENHOFER > Nosticova 2, tram #12, #20 or #22 to Hellichova ☏ 257 316 830, Ⓦ www.dientzenhofer.cz. MAP P.48-49, POCKET MAP D12. Birthplace of the eponymous architect Kilian Ignác Dientzenhofer and a very popular and unpretentious pension, as it's one of the few reasonably priced places (anywhere in Prague) to have wheelchair access. **Doubles from 3200Kč**.

DŮM U VELKÉ BOTY (THE BIG SHOE) > Vlašská 30, tram #12, #20 or #22 to Malostranské náměstí ☏ 257 532 088, Ⓦ www.dumuvelkeboty.cz. MAP P.48-49, POCKET MAP B12. The sheer discreetness of this pension, in a lovely old building in the quiet backstreets, is one of its main draws. Run by a very friendly couple, who speak good English, it has a series of cosy rooms, replete with genuine antiques, some en suite, some not. Breakfast is extra, but worth it. **Doubles from 3000Kč**.

LUNDBORG > U Lužického semináře 3, tram #12, #20 or #22 to Malostranské náměstí ☏ 257 011 911, Ⓦ www .lundborg.cz. MAP P.48-49, POCKET MAP D12. Very stylish Swedish-run apartment suites with Baroque painted ceilings and tasteful furnishings, as well as jacuzzis and free internet access in every room. Situated in the thick of it, right by the Charles Bridge tower. **Suites from 6000Kč**.

NERUDA > Nerudova 44, tram #12, #20 or #22 to Malostranské náměstí ☏ 257 535 557, Ⓦ www .hotelneruda-praha.cz. MAP P.48-49, POCKET MAP B11. Stylish hotel a fair walk up Nerudova, with a funky, glass-roofed foyer, lots of natural stone, and smart, minimalist modern decor in the rooms. **Doubles from 3000Kč**.

NOSTICOVA > Nosticova 1, tram #12, #20 or #22 to Hellichova ☏ 257 312 513, Ⓦ www.nosticova.com. MAP P.48-49, POCKET MAP D12. Baroque house with ten beautifully restored apartments replete with antique furnishings, sumptuous bathrooms and small kitchens, on a peaceful square not far from the Charles Bridge. **Apartments from 7500Kč**.

SAX > Janský vršek 3, tram #12, #20 or #22 to Malostranské náměstí ☏ 257 531 268, Ⓦ www.hotelsax.cz. MAP P.48-49, POCKET MAP C12. Perfectly located in the backstreets off Nerudova, this hotel has gone for a remarkably convincing groovy retro 1960s look, but it's also very well-run, well-equipped place with a DVD library and free wi-fi. **Doubles from 3500Kč**.

U KARLOVA MOSTU > Na Kampě 15, tram #12, #20 or #22 to Malostranské náměstí ☎ 234 652 808, Ⓦ www .archibald.cz. MAP P.48–49, POCKET MAP E12. Situated on a lovely tree-lined square, just off the Charles Bridge, the rooms in this former brewery (now a pub-restaurant) have real character, despite the modern fittings. **Doubles from 5500Kč.**

U MODRÉHO KLÍČE (BLUE KEY) > Letenská 14, metro Malostranská ☎ 257 534 361. MAP P.48–49, POCKET MAP D11. Friendly, swish, blue-themed hotel in a good location (despite the busy road outside), just a short stroll from Malostranské náměstí; ask for a room facing into the lovely courtyard. **Doubles from 3000Kč.**

U PÁVA (THE PEACOCK) > U lužického semináře 32, metro Malostranská ☎ 257 533 360, Ⓦ www .romantichotels.cz. MAP P.48–49, POCKET MAP E11. Tucked away in the quiet backstreets, *U páva* boasts some sumptuously over-the-top Baroque fittings – real and repro. Some rooms have views over to the castle and service is good. **Doubles from 3000Kč.**

U ZLATÉ STUDNĚ (THE GOLDEN WELL) > U zlaté studně 4, tram #12, #20 or #22 to Malostranské náměstí ☎ 257 011 213, Ⓦ www.goldenwell .cz. MAP P.48–49, POCKET MAP D11. The location is pretty special: tucked into the terraces below Prague Castle, next to the terraced gardens, with incredible views across the rooftops. The rooms aren't half bad either, with lots of original ceilings, and there's a good restaurant attached, with a wonderful summer terrace. **Doubles from 4500Kč.**

U ZLATÝCH NŮŽEK (THE GOLDEN SCISSORS) > Na Kampě 6, tram #12, #20 or #22 to Malostranské náměstí ☎ 5257 530 473, Ⓦ www .uzlatychnuzek.com. MAP P.48–49, POCKET MAP E12. Ten pleasant rooms with parquet flooring, the odd beam and simple modern furnishings on Kampa island, close to the Charles Bridge. **Doubles from 2875Kč.**

Staré Město

ARCADIA OLD TOWN > Kožná 6 and 13, metro Můstek ☎ 224 922 040, Ⓦ www.arcadiaoldtown.com. MAP P.62–63, POCKET MAP G12. A cosy set of apartments right in the heart of the labyrinth of streets south of Old Town Square. Decor is bright, cheerful and modern. **Apartments from 3400Kč.**

ČERNÁ LIŠKA (THE BLACK FOX) > Mikulášská 2, metro Staroměstská ☎ 224 232 250, Ⓦ www.cernaliska .cz. MAP P.62–63, POCKET MAP G12. So central it's ridiculous, yet with friendly and helpful staff; well-appointed rooms, all with lovely wooden floors, some with incredible views onto Old Town Square, and quieter ones at the back. **Doubles from 3700Kč.**

ČERNÝ SLON (BLACK ELEPHANT) > Týnská 1, metro Náměstí Republiky ☎ 222 321 521, Ⓦ www .hotelcernyslon.cz. MAP P.62–63, POCKET MAP G11. Another ancient building tucked away off Old Town Square by the north portal of the Týn church, now tastefully converted into a very comfortable small hotel. **Doubles from 3900Kč.**

CLOISTER INN Konviktská 14, metro Národní třída ☎ 224 211 020, Ⓦ www.cloister-inn.com. MAP P.62–63, POCKET MAP F13. Pleasant, well-equipped hotel housed in a nunnery in one of the backstreets; the rooms are simply furnished with modern fittings, free wi-fi, and the location is good. **Doubles from 2500Kč.**

GRAND HOTEL BOHEMIA > Kralodvorská 4, metro Náměstí Republiky ☎ 234 608 111, Ⓦ www.grandhotelbohemia.cz. MAP.62–63, POCKET MAP H12. Probably the most elegant luxury hotel in the old town, just behind the Obecní dům, with some very tasty Art Nouveau decor and all the amenities you'd expect from an Austrian outfit. **Doubles from 3500Kč.**

GRAND HOTEL PRAHA > Staroměstské náměstí 22, metro Můstek ☎ 221 632 556, ⓦ www.grandhotelpraha.cz. MAP P.62–63, POCKET MAP G12. If you want a room overlooking the astronomical clock on Old Town Square, then book in here, well in advance. There are beautiful antique furnishings, big oak ceilings, but only a very few rooms, including a single, as well as an attic suite for four. **Doubles from 4000Kč.**

HOSTEL TÝN > Týnská 19, metro Náměstí Republiky ☎ 224 828 519, ⓦ www.hosteltyn.com. MAP P.62–63, POCKET MAP H11. Prague's most centrally located hostel is a very basic affair, located in a quiet courtyard (with a veggie Indian café in it) a stone's throw from Old Town Square. **Doubles from 1240Kč, five-bed dorms 420Kč.**

JOSEF > Rybná 20, metro Náměstí Republiky ☎ 221 700 111, ⓦ www .hoteljosef.com. MAP P.62–63, POCKET MAP H11. Staré Město's top designer hotel exudes modern professionalism, the lobby is a symphony in off-white efficiency and the rooms continue the crisply maintained minimalist theme. **Doubles from 3500Kč.**

PACHTŮV PALACE > Karoliny Světlé 34, metro Národní třída ☎ 234 705 111, ⓦ www.pachtuvpalace.com. MAP P.62–63, POCKET MAP F12. Former Baroque palace, now luxury hotel, in the heart of the old town, with charming and efficient staff, rooms and suites decked in a blend of antique and repro furniture. **Doubles from 5000Kč.**

RESIDENCE ŘETĚZOVÁ > Řetězová 9, metro Staroměstská ☎ 222 221 800, ⓦ www.retezova.com. MAP P.62–63, POCKET MAP F12. Attractive apartments of all sizes, with kitchenettes, wooden or stone floors, Gothic vaulting or wooden beams and repro furnishings throughout. **Apartments from 3000Kč.**

RITCHIE'S HOSTEL > Karlova 9 and 13, metro Staroměstská ☎ 222 221 229, ⓦ www.ritchieshostel.cz. MAP P.62–63, POCKET MAP F12. In the midst of the human river that is Karlova, this Old Town hostel is clean, with accommodation ranging from en-suite doubles to twelve-bed dorms; no in-house laundry or cooking facilities. **Doubles from 1500Kč, dorm beds 300Kč.**

SAVIC > Jilská 7, metro Národní třída ☎ 224 248 555, ⓦ www.savic.eu. MAP P.62–63, POCKET MAP G12. This hotel, in the heart of the old town, has retained plenty of period features: painted ceilings, vaulting, exposed beams and the like. Staff are as helpful as can be and the buffet breakfast is superb. **Doubles from 4000Kč.**

TRAVELLERS HOSTEL > Dlouhá 33, metro Náměstí Republiky ☎ 224 826 662, ⓦ www.travellers.cz. MAP P.62–63, POCKET MAP H11. Very centrally located party hostel (although it's not the cleanest of places), situated above the *Roxy* nightclub, and the main booking office for a network of hostels – if there's not enough room here, staff will find you a bed in one of their other central branches. **Dorm beds from 300Kč, doubles from 1400Kč.**

U MEDVÍDKŮ (THE LITTLE BEARS) > Na Perštýně 7, metro Národní třída ☎ 224 211 916, ⓦ www.umedvidku .cz. MAP P.62–63, POCKET MAP G13.The rooms above this famous Prague pub are plainly furnished, quiet considering the locale, and therefore something of an Old Town bargain; booking ahead essential. **Doubles from 3500Kč.**

UNITAS > Bartolomějská 9, metro Národní třída. ☎ 224 230 603, ⓦ art-prison.prague-hostels.cz. MAP P.62–63, POCKET MAP F13. Set in a Franciscan nunnery, the *Unitas* offers both simple twins and bargain dorm beds in the converted secret police prison cells of its *Art Prison Hostel* (Havel was kept in P6). **Twins from 1260Kč; doubles from 2000Kč.**

U TŘÍ BUBNŮ (THE THREE DRUMS) > U radnice 8–10, metro Staroměstská ☎ 224 214 855, ⓦ www.utribubnu .cz. MAP P.62–63, POCKET MAP G12. Small hotel just off Old Town Square with five tastefully furnished rooms, either with original fifteenth-century wooden ceilings or lots of exposed beams. No lift but plenty of stairs. Free wi-fi. **Doubles from 3600Kč.**

Wenceslas Square and northern Nové Město

ALCRON > Štěpánská 40, metro Můstek or Muzeum ☎ 222 820 000, Ⓦ www.radissonblu.com. MAP P.88, POCKET MAP H14. Giant 1930s luxury hotel, just off Wenceslas Square, which has been superbly restored to its former Art Deco glory by the Radisson chain. Double rooms here are without doubt the most luxurious and tasteful you'll find in Nové Město. Free wi-fi. **Doubles from 5000Kč.**

EVROPA > Václavské náměstí 25, metro Můstek ☎ 224 215 387, Ⓦ www .evropahotel.cz. MAP P.88, POCKET MAP H13. Sumptuously decorated in Art Nouveau style, and potentially the most wonderful hotel in Prague, this place is still run like an old Communist behemoth – a blast from the past in every sense. The doubles with shared facilities (and without breakfast) on the student floor are only 800Kč each. **En-suite doubles from 1600Kč.**

HOSTEL ROSEMARY > Růžová 5, metro Můstek or Hlavní nádraží ☎ 222 211 124, Ⓦ www.praguecityhostel .cz. MAP P.88, POCKET MAP J13. Clean, modern hostel a short walk from the main train station, Praha hlavní nádraží. Three- to twelve-bed mixed dorms, plus doubles with or without en-suite/kitchen facilities. Communal kitchen and free internet. **Dorms from 400Kč; doubles from 1300Kč.**

IMPERIAL > Na poříčí 15, metro Náměstí Republiky ☎ 246 011 600, Ⓦ www.hotel-imperial.cz. MAP P.88, POCKET MAP J11. Despite describing itself as Art Deco, this place is actually more of an Art Nouveau masterpiece. Built in 1914, the public rooms are dripping with period ceramic friezes; the rest of the hotel is standard twenty-first-century luxury. **Doubles from 5500Kč.**

PALACE > Panská 12, metro Můstek ☎ 224 093 111, Ⓦ www.palacehotel .cz. MAP P.88, POCKET MAP H13. Luxury five-star hotel just off Wenceslas Square, renowned for its excellent service and facilities – rooms are spotless and the buffet breakfast is top-class. **Doubles from 4500Kč.**

PAŘÍŽ > U Obecního domu 1, metro Náměstí Republiky ☎ 222 195 195, Ⓦ www.hotel-paris.cz. MAP P.88, POCKET MAP H11. This is a good top-notch hotel with plenty of *fin de siècle* atmosphere surviving – it was the setting for Bohumil Hrabal's *I Served the King of England*. **Doubles from 4500Kč.**

SALVATOR > Truhlářská 10, metro Náměstí Republiky ☎ 222 312 234, Ⓦ www.salvator.cz. MAP P.88, POCKET MAP J11. Very good location for the price, just a minute's walk from náměstí Republiky, with small but clean rooms (the cheaper ones with shared facilities), set around a courtyard. Good buffet breakfast, friendly staff and free wi-fi. **Doubles from 2300Kč.**

Národní and southern Nové Město

HOTEL 16 – U SV KATEŘINY > Kateřinská 16, tram #18 or #24 ☎ 224 920 636, Ⓦ www.hotel16 .cz. MAP P.97, POCKET MAP E7. Really friendly, family-run hotel offering small, plain but clean en-suite rooms. There's a small terraced garden at the back and botanic gardens nearby. **Doubles from 2900Kč.**

ICON HOTEL > V jámě 6, metro Můstek ☎ 221 634 100, Ⓦ www .iconhotel.eu. MAP P.97, POCKET MAP H14. Modern designer hotel, whose white-walled rooms are equipped with large, handmade Hästens beds. All day à la carte breakfast will suit late risers. **Doubles from 4700Kč.**

KLUB HABITAT > Na Zderaze 10, metro Karlovo náměstí ☎ 224 918 252, Ⓦ web.telecom.cz/habitat. MAP P.97, POCKET MAP F15. Perfectly serviceable, clean, charity-run hostel in a great location south of Národní. Breakfast included; free internet. **Dorm beds from 450Kč.**

MISS SOPHIE'S > Melounová 3, metro I. P. Pavlova ☎ 296 303 530, Ⓦ www.miss-sophies.com. MAP P.97, POCKET MAP E7. The most central of Prague's smart new designer hostels, offering everything from cheap dorm beds to fully equipped apartments. **Dorm beds from 400Kč, doubles from 1790Kč.**

NA ZLATÉM KŘÍŽI (GOLDEN CROSS) > Jungmannovo náměstí 2, metro Můstek ☎ 224 219 501, Ⓦ www .antikhotels.com. MAP P.97, POCKET MAP G13. Small hotel in a very tall (no lift), narrow building just a step away from the bottom of Wenceslas Square. Rooms are spacious – especially the suites – and decked out in tasteful modern furnishings. **Doubles from 2500Kč..**

U ŠUTERŮ > Palackého 4, metro Můstek ☎ 224 948 235, Ⓦ www .usuteru.cz. MAP P.97, POCKET MAP G14. With elegant modern furnishings, wooden floors, and some lovely vaulted ceiling, this small pension is a very good-value choice in a decent location between Národní and Wenceslas Square. Staff are very helpful and the downstairs restaurant is great. **Doubles from 2400Kč.**

Vyšehrad, Vinohrady and Žižkov

ALPIN > Velehradská 25, metro Jiřího z Poděbrad ☎ 222 723 982, Ⓦ www .alpin.cz. MAP P.109, POCKET MAP G6. Clean, bare, bargain basement rooms on the border between Vinohrady and Žižkov; it's a short hop on the tram or metro to get into town. **Doubles from 1700Kč.**

ANNA > Budečská 17, metro Náměstí Míru ☎ 222 513 111, Ⓦ www .hotelanna.cz. MAP P.109, POCKET MAP F7. Plain, but smartly appointed

rooms, warm friendly staff and a decent location make this a popular choice in Vinohrady, with trams and the metro close by. Free wi-fi. **Doubles from 2500Kč**

ARCADIA > Hostivítova 33, tram #3, #7, #16, #17 and #21 ☎ 224 922 040 Ⓦ www.arcadiaresidence.com. MAP P.109, POCKET MAP D8. Spacious series of apartments at the foot of Vyšehrad, all really beautifully furnished with stylish pieces of period furniture. The owners couldn't be more charming and it's only a short trip on the tram into town. **Apartments from 2600Kč.**

CLOWN AND BARD > Bořivojova 102, tram #5, #9 or #26 to Husinecká ☎ 222 716 453, Ⓦ www.clownandbard .com. MAP P.109, POCKET MAP G6. Žižkov hostel that attracts backpackers who like to party. Still, it's clean, undeniably cheap, stages events and has laundry facilities and free wi-fi. Veggie breakfast extra. **Dorm beds from 300Kč, doubles from 1200Kč.**

CZECH INN > Francouzská 76, tram #4, #22 ☎ 267 267 600, Ⓦ www .czech-inn.com. MAP P.109, POCKET MAP G8. Upbeat, designer hostel that feels and looks like a hotel, with friendly and helpful staff and a choice of dormitories and private rooms. **Dorm beds from 400Kč, doubles from 1600Kč.**

GALILEO > Bruselská 3, tram #6 or #11 to Bruselská ☎ 222 500 222, Ⓦ www.hotel-galileo-prague.com. MAP P.109, POCKET MAP F7. Chic, modern hotel furnished with style, offering apartments as well as en-suite doubles. **Doubles from 2600Kč.**

Arrival

Prague is one of Europe's smaller capital cities. The airport lies just over 10km northwest of the city centre, with only a bus link or taxi to get you into town. Both the international train stations and the main bus terminal are linked to the centre by the fast and efficient metro system.

By plane

Prague's **Ruzyně airport** (☎ 220 113 314, ⓦ www.pragueairport.co.uk) is connected to the city by minibus, bus and taxi. The Cedaz (ⓦ www.cedaz.cz) shared **minibus** service will take you (and several others) to your hotel for around 480Kč. The minibus also runs a scheduled service (daily 7.30am–7pm; every 30min), which stops first at Dejvická metro station (journey time 20min), and ends up at V celnici, off náměstí Republiky (journey time 30min); the full journey currently costs 120Kč. Another option is the **Prague Airport Shuttle** (ⓦ www.prague-airport-shuttle.com) which will take you into town for 550Kč for up to four passengers.

The cheapest way to get into town is on local **bus #119** (daily 5am–midnight; every 15–20min; journey time 25min), which stops frequently and also ends its journey outside Dejvická metro station. You can buy your ticket from the public transport (DP) information desk in arrivals (daily 7am–10pm), or from the nearby machines or newsagents. If you're going to use public transport whilst in Prague, you might as well buy a pass straight away (see opposite). If you arrive between midnight and 5am, you can catch the hourly **night bus** #510 to Divoká Šárka, the terminus for night tram #51, which will take you on to Národní in the centre of town. Another cheap alternative is **Linka AE** (Airport Express), a non-stop bus link with Dejvická metro (30Kč) and Praha hlavní nádraží (daily 7am–9pm; every 30min; 50Kč).

If you're thinking of taking a **taxi** from the airport into the centre, choose AAA Taxi (☎ 14014, ⓦ www .aaataxi.cz), as Prague taxi drivers have a reputation for overcharging. AAA have a rank outside arrivals and the journey to the city centre should cost around 400–500Kč.

By train

International trains arrive either at Praha hlavní nádraží, on the edge of Nové Město and Vinohrady, or at Praha-Holešovice, which lies north of the city centre. At both stations you'll find exchange outlets, 24hr left-luggage offices (úschovna zavazadel) and accommodation agencies (plus a tourist office at Hlavní nádraží). Both stations are on metro lines, and Hlavní nádraží is only a five-minute walk from Václavské náměstí (Wenceslas Square).

By bus

Prague's **main bus terminal** is Praha-Florenc (metro Florenc), on the eastern edge of Nové Město, where virtually all long-distance international and domestic services terminate. It's a confusing place to end up, but it has a left-luggage office upstairs (daily 5am–11pm), and you can make a quick exit to the adjacent metro station.

Getting around

The centre of Prague is reasonably small and best explored on foot. At some point, however, particularly to reach some of the more widely dispersed attractions, you'll need to use the city's cheap and efficient public transport system (*dopravní podnik* or DP; ⓦ www.dpp.cz), which comprises the metro and a network of trams and buses. You can get free maps, tickets and passes from the DP **information offices** (☎ 800 191 817) at both airport terminals (daily 7am–10pm), from Holešovice train station (Mon–Fri 7am–6pm), Můstek metro (Mon–Fri 7am–6pm), Muzeum metro (daily 7am–9pm) and Anděl metro (Mon–Fri 7am–9pm).

Tickets and passes

Most Praguers buy monthly passes, and to avoid having to understand the complexities of the single ticket system, you too are best off buying a **travel pass** (*jízdenka*) for either 24 hours (*1 den*; 100Kč), three days (*3 dny*; 330Kč), or five days (*5 dny*; 500Kč); no photos or ID are needed, though you must punch it to validate when you first use it. All the passes are available from DP outlets and ticket machines.

Despite the multitude of buttons on the **ticket machines** – found inside all metro stations and at some bus and tram stops – there are just two basic choices. The 18Kč version (*limitovaná*) allows you to travel for 20 minutes on the trams or buses, or up to five stops on the metro; it's also known as a *nepřestupní jízdenka*, or "no change ticket", although you can in fact change metro lines (but not buses or trams). The 26Kč version (*základní*) is valid for 75 minutes during which you may change trams, buses or metro lines

as many times as you like, hence its name, *přestupní jízdenka*, or "changing ticket". A full price ticket is called *plnocenná*; discounted tickets (*zvýhodněna*) are available for children aged 6–15; under-6s travel free.

To buy a ticket from one of the machines, press the appropriate button followed by the *výdej*/enter button, then put your money in. The machines do give change, but if you don't have enough coins, the person on duty in the metro office by the barriers can give you change or sell you a ticket. Tickets can also be bought from a tobacconist (*tabák*), street kiosk, newsagent, PIS office or any place that displays the yellow DP sticker. When you enter the metro, or board a tram or bus, you must validate your ticket in one of the machines to hand.

There are no barriers, but plain-clothes inspectors (*revizoři*) make random checks and will issue an on-the-spot fine of 700Kč to anyone caught without a valid ticket or pass; controllers should show you their ID (a small metal disc) and give you a receipt (*paragon*).

Metro

Prague's futuristic, Soviet-built **metro** is fast, smooth and ultra-clean, running daily 5am till midnight with trains every two minutes during peak hours, slowing down to every four to ten minutes by late evening. Its three lines intersect at various points in the city centre. The stations are fairly discreetly marked above ground with the metro logo, in green (line A), yellow (line B) or red (line C). Inside the metro, *výstup* means exit and *přestup* will lead you to one of the connecting lines. The digital clock at the end of the platform tells you what time it is and how long it was since the last train.

Trams

The electric tram (*tramvaj*) system negotiates Prague's hills and cobbles with remarkable dexterity. Modern rolling stock is gradually being introduced, but most of Prague's trams (traditionally red and cream) date back to the Communist era. After the metro, trams are the fastest and most efficient way of getting around, running every 6–8min at peak times, and every 5–15min at other times – check the timetables posted at every stop (*zastávka*), which list the departure times from that stop. Note that it is the custom for younger folk (and men of all ages) to vacate their seat when an older woman enters the carriage.

Tram #22, which runs from Vinohrady to Hradčany via the centre of town and Malá Strana, is a good, cheap way of sightseeing, though you should beware of pickpockets. From March to November, nostalgic tram #91 runs from the Transport Museum to Výstaviště, via Prague Castle, Malá Strana , Wenceslas Square and náměstí Republiky and back again (Sat & Sun hourly noon–5.30pm; 40min; 35Kč). **Night trams** (*noční tramvaje*; #51–58; every 30–40min; roughly midnight–4.30am) run on different routes from the daytime ones, though at some point all night trams pass along Lazarská in Nové Město.

Buses

You'll rarely need to get on a **bus** (*autobus*) in Prague, since most of them keep well out of the centre. If you're intent upon visiting the zoo, staying in one of the city's more obscure suburbs, or taking the cheap option to the airport, you will need to use them: their hours of operation are similar to those of the trams (though generally less frequent). **Night buses** (*noční autobusy*) run once an hour midnight–5am.

Ferries and boats

The public transport system runs a handful of small summer **ferry services** (*přívoz*) on the Vltava between the islands and the riverbanks (April–Oct daily 6am–10pm every 30min). In the summer months there are also regular boat trips on the River Vltava run by the PPS (Pražská paroplavební společnost; ☎ 224 930 017, ⓦ www .paroplavba.cz) from just south of Jiráskův most on Rašínovo nábřeží. Three or four boats a day in summer run to Troja (see p.123) in the northern suburbs (May to mid-Sept daily; April & mid-Sept to Oct Sat and Sun only; 220Kč return).

The PPS also offers boat trips around Prague (April to mid-Sept daily 1–2hr; 220–290Kč) on board a 1930s paddlesteamer. Another option is to hop aboard the much smaller boats run by Pražské Benátky/Prague-Venice (☎ 776 776 779, ⓦ www .prazskebenatky.cz), which depart year round for a half-hour meander over to the Čertovka by Kampa island (300Kč). The boats leave from the north side of the Charles Bridge on the Staré Město bank.

Taxis

Taxis are, theoretically at least, relatively cheap. However, many Prague taxi drivers will attempt to overcharge, particularly at taxi ranks close to the tourist sights. Officially, the initial fare on the meter should be around 40Kč plus 28Kč/km within Prague and 6Kč/min waiting time. The best advice is to have your hotel or pension call you one – you then qualify for a cheaper rate – rather than hail one or pick one up at the taxi ranks. The cab company with the best reputation is AAA Taxi (☎ 14014, ⓦ www.aaataxi.cz), which has metered taxis all over Prague.

Directory A–Z

Addresses

The street name is always written before the building number in Prague addresses. The city is divided into numbered postal districts: of the areas covered in the guide, central Prague is Prague 1; southern Nové Město and half of Vinohrady is Prague 2; the rest of Vinohrady and Žižkov is Prague 3; Holešovice is Prague 7.

Bike rental

City Bike, Královdorská 5. April–Oct daily 9am–7pm; ☎776 180 284, ⓦ www.citybike-prague.com; metro Náměstí Republiky.

Children

Despite a friendly attitude to kids and babies in general, you'll see very few children in museums and galleries, or in pubs, restaurants or cafés. Apart from the zoo and the mirror maze, there aren't very many attractions specifically aimed at kids. The castle and the Petřín funicular usually go down well, as does a ride on a tram.

Cinema

Cinema tickets still cost less than 100Kč. Most films are shown in the original language with subtitles (*titulky* or *české titulky*); some blockbusters are dubbed (dabing or *česká verze*). Occasionally you can get to see a Czech film with English subtitles (*anglický titulky*).

Crime

There are two main types of police: the **Policie** are the national force with white shirts, navy blue jackets and grey trousers, while the **Městská** policie, run by the Prague city authorities, are distinguishable by their all-black uniforms. The main central police station is at Bartolomějská 6, Staré Město.

Cultural institutes

American Center, Tržiště13 ⓦ prague.usembassy.gov; **Austrian Cultural Institute**, Jungmannovo náměstí 18 ⓦ www.bmeia.gv.at; **Instituto Cervantes Bredovský dvůr**, Na rybníčku 6 ⓦ www.cervantes.cz; **Goethe Institut**, Masarykovo nábřeží 32 ⓦ www.goethe.de/prag; **Institut Français**, Štěpánská 35 ⓦ www.ifp.cz; **Instituto Italiano di Cultura**, Šporkova 14 ⓦ www.iicpraga.esteri.it.

Disabilities

The guidebook *Accessible Prague/ Přístupná Praha* is available from the Prague Wheelchair Association (Pražská organizace vozíčkářů), Benediktská 6 ☎224 827 210, ⓦ www.pov.cz.

Electricity

The standard continental 220 volts AC. Most European appliances should work as long as you have an adaptor for continental-style two-pin round plugs. North Americans will need this plus a transformer.

Embassies

Australia, Klimentská 10, Nové Město ☎251 018 350; **Canada**, Muchova 6, Bubeneč ☎272 101 890, ⓦ www.canada.cz; **Ireland**, Tržiště 13, Malá Strana ☎257 530 061; **New Zealand**, Dykova 19, Vinohrady ☎222 514 672; **UK**, Thunovská 14, Malá Strana ☎257 402 111, ⓦ ukinczechrepublic.fco.gov.uk; **US**, Tržiště 15, Malá Strana ☎257 530 663, ⓦ www.usembassy.cz.

Emergencies

☎112; Ambulance ☎155; Police ☎158; Fire ☎150.

Gay and lesbian Prague

There's a small but well-established gay and lesbian scene with its spiritual heart in the leafy suburbs of Vinohrady and the more rundown neighbourhood of Žižkov. Up-to-date listings are available from ⓦ prague.gayguide.net.

Health

For an English-speaking doctor, go to Nemocnice na Homolce, Roentgenova 2, Motol (☎ 257 271 111). If it's an emergency, dial ☎ 155 for an ambulance. For an emergency dentist, head for Palackého 5, Nové Město; metro Můstek (☎ 224 946 981). For a 24hr chemist, try Palackého 5 (☎ 224 946 982) or Belgická 37 (☎ 222 513 396).

Internet

Plenty of Prague's hotels and cafés have free wi-fi – if you don't have a laptop, head for the *Globe* (see p.104).

Left luggage

Prague's main bus and train stations have lockers and/or a 24hr left-luggage office, with instructions in English.

Lost property

The main train stations have lost property offices – look for the sign *ztráty a nálezy* – and there's a central municipal one at Karoliny Světlé 5 (Mon–Fri only). If you've lost your passport, then get in touch with your embassy (see p.139).

Money

The currency is the Czech crown or koruna česká (abbreviated to Kč or CZK). At the time of going to press there were roughly 30Kč to the pound sterling, 25Kč to the euro and around 20Kč to the US dollar. For up-to-date exchange rates, consult ⓦ www.oanda.com or ⓦ www.xe.com. Notes come in 20Kč, 50Kč, 100Kč, 200Kč, 500Kč, 1000Kč and 2000Kč (and less frequently 5000Kč) denominations; coins as 1Kč, 2Kč, 5Kč, 10Kč, 20Kč and 50Kč. Banking hours are Monday–Friday 8am–5pm, often with a break at lunchtime. ATMs can be found across the city.

Newspapers

You can get most foreign dailies and magazines at the kiosks at the bottom of Wenceslas Square, outside metro Můstek.

Opening hours

Shops in Prague are generally open Monday–Friday 9am–5pm, though most tourist shops stay open until 6pm or later. Some shops close by noon or 1pm on Saturday and close all day Sunday, but there's no law against opening on Sundays and many shops in the centre do (including both main supermarkets/department stores). Museums and galleries are generally open Tuesday–Sunday 10am–6pm.

Phones

Most public phones take only phone cards (*telefonní karty*), available from post offices, tobacconists and some shops (prices vary). The best-value ones are pre-paid phone cards that give you a phone number and a code to enter. There are instructions in English, and if you press the appropriate button the language on the digital read-out will change to English. If you have any problems, ring ☎ 1181 to get through to international information. Nearly all Prague phone numbers are nine-digit. There are no separate city/area codes in the Czech Republic.

Post

The main 24hr post office (pošta) is at Jindřišská 14, Nové Město ☎ 0800 104 4120; take a ticket and wait for your number to come up. A more tourist-friendly branch exists in the third courtyard of Prague Castle.

The Prague Card

The Prague Card (ⓦ www.praguecard .biz) is valid for four days and gives free entry into over fifty sights for 740Kč (though not including the sights of the former Ghetto of Josefov); for an extra 220Kč it also includes a travel pass. All in all, the card will save you a lot of hassle, but not necessarily that much money. The card is available from all travel information and PIS offices.

Smoking

The Czechs have yet to give in to the EU trend of banning smoking in pubs and restaurants, though a no-smoking area should be provided.

Time

The Czech Republic is on Central European Time (CET), one hour ahead of Britain and six hours ahead of EST, with the clocks going forward in spring and back again some time in autumn – the exact date changes from year to year. Generally speaking, Czechs use the 24-hour clock.

Tipping

Tipping is normal practice in cafés, bars, restaurants and taxis, though it is usually done simply by rounding up the total. For example, if the waiter tots up the bill and asks you for 138Kč, you should give him 150Kč and tell him to keep the change. Automatic service charges that appear on the bill are not a standard Czech practice.

Toilets

Apart from the automatic ones in central Prague, public toilets (záchody, toalety or WC) are few and far between. In some, you have to buy toilet paper (by the sheet) from the attendant, whom you will also have to pay as you enter. Standards of hygiene can be low. Gentlemen should head for muži or páni; ladies should head for ženy or dámy.

Tourist information

The tourist office is the **Prague Information Service** or PIS (Pražská informační služba), whose main branch is within the **Staroměstská radnice** on Staroměstské náměstí (April–Oct Mon–Fri 9am–7pm, Sat & Sun 9am–6pm; Nov–March Mon–Fri 9am–6pm, Sat & Sun 9am–5pm; ⓦ www.prague-info.cz). There are additional PIS offices at **Rytířská 31**, Staré Město (metro Můstek), in the **main train station**, Praha hlavní nádraží, plus an (April–Oct only) office in the **Malá Strana bridge tower** on the Charles Bridge. PIS staff speak English, but their helpfulness varies enormously; however, they can usually answer most enquiries, and can organize accommodation, sell maps, guides and theatre tickets.

PIS also distributes and sells some useful **listings publications**, including Culture in Prague/Česká kultura (ⓦ www.ceskakultura.cz), a monthly English-language booklet listing the major events, concerts and exhibitions; Přehled, a more comprehensive monthly listings magazine (in Czech only); and the weekly English-language newspaper, Prague Post (ⓦ www.praguepost .com), which carries selective listings.

The best **website** for finding your way around the capital is ⓦ www .mapy.cz, which will help you locate any hotel, restaurant, pub, shop or street in Prague. A more general, informative site is Radio Prague's ⓦ www.radio.cz/english. with the latest news and weather.

Festivals and events

EPIPHANY (TŘÍ KRÁLOVÉ)

January 6

The letters K + M + B followed by the date of the new year are chalked on doorways across the capital to celebrate the "Day of the Three Kings" when the Magi came to worship Christ.

DAYS OF EUROPEAN FILM (DNY EVROPSKÉHO FILMU)

Late January/early February
Ⓦ www.eurofilmfest.cz
This is the nearest Prague comes to a film festival: a fortnight of arty European films shown at various screens across the capital.

MASOPUST OR CARNEVALE

Shrove Tuesday
The approach of Masopust (the Czech version of Mardi Gras) is celebrated locally in the Žižkov district of Prague, where there's a five-day programme of parties, concerts and parades; a more mainstream series of events takes place under the umbrella of Carnevale, in the city centre.

EASTER (VELIKONOCE)

The age-old sexist ritual of whipping girls' calves with braided birch twigs tied together with ribbons (*pomlázky*) is still practised outside of Prague. To prevent such a fate, the girls are supposed to offer the boys a coloured Easter egg and pour a bucket of cold water over them. You'll see *pomlázky* and Easter eggs on sale, but precious little whipping.

"BURNING OF THE WITCHES" (PÁLENÍ ČARODĚJNIC)

April 30
Halloween comes early to the Czech Republic when bonfires are lit across the country, and old brooms thrown out and burned, as everyone celebrates the end of the long winter.

PRAGUE INTERNATIONAL MARATHON

Early May Ⓦ www.praguemarathon.com.
Runners from over fifty countries come to race through the city's cobbled streets and over the Charles Bridge.

PRAGUE SPRING FESTIVAL (PRAŽSKÉ JARO)

May 12–June 2 Box office at Hellichova 18, Malá Strana, ☎ 257 312 547, Ⓦ www.festival.cz.
By far the biggest annual arts event and the country's most prestigious international music festival. Established in 1946, it traditionally begins on May 12, the anniversary of Smetana's death, with a procession from his grave in Vyšehrad to the Obecní dům where the composer's *Má vlast* (My Country) is performed in the presence of the president, finishing on June 2 with a rendition of Beethoven's *Ninth Symphony*. Tickets for the festival sell out fast – try your luck by writing, a month before the festival begins.

WORLD ROMA FESTIVAL (KHAMORO)

Late May Ⓦ www.khamoro.cz.
International Roma festival of music, dance and film, plus seminars and workshops.

WORLD FESTIVAL OF PUPPET ART

Late May/early June Ⓦ www.puppetart.com.
A week-long international puppet festival organized by Prague's chief puppetry institute.

RESPECT FESTIVAL

June Ⓦ www.respectmusic.cz.
This world music weekend is held at various venues across the city in June, including the Akropolis and Štvanice island.

DANCE PRAGUE (TANEC PRAHA)

Three weeks in June Ⓦ www.tanecpha.cz
An established highlight of Prague's cultural calendar, this international festival of modern dance takes place over three weeks in June throughout the city.

BURČÁK

Two weeks, end of September
For a couple of weeks, temporary stalls on street corners sell the year's partially fermented new wine, known as *burčák*, a misty, heady brew.

CHRISTMAS MARKETS

Christmas markets selling gifts, food and mulled wine (*svařák*) are set up at several places around the city in December: the biggest ones are on Wenceslas Square and the Old Town Square. Temporary ice rinks are also constructed at various locations.

SAINT BARBARA

December 4
On the saint's feast day, cherry-tree branches are bought as decorations, the aim being to get them to blossom before Christmas.

EVE OF ST NICHOLAS

December 5
On the evening of December 5,

Public holidays

January 1 New Year's Day; **Easter Monday**; **May 1** May Day; **May 8** VE Day; **July 5** Introduction of Christianity; **July 6** Death of Jan Hus; **September 28** Czech State Day; **October 28** Foundation of the Republic; **November 17** Battle for Freedom and Democracy Day; **December 24** Christmas Eve; **December 25** Christmas Day; **December 26** St Stephen's Day

numerous trios, dressed up as St Nicholas (svatý Mikuláš), an angel and a devil, tour round the streets, the angel handing out sweets and fruit to children who've been good, while the devil dishes out coal and potatoes to those who've been naughty. The Czech St Nicholas has white hair and a beard, and dresses not in red but in a white priest's outfit, with a bishop's mitre.

BOHUSLAV MARTINŮ FESTIVAL

Early December Ⓦ www.martinu.cz.
Annual festival of music in early December celebrating the least well-known of the big four Czech composers.

CHRISTMAS EVE (ŠTĚDRÝ VEČER)

December 24 is traditionally a day of fasting, broken only when the evening star appears, signalling the beginning of the Christmas feast of carp, potato salad, schnitzel and sweetbreads. Only after the meal are the children allowed to open their presents, which miraculously appear beneath the tree, thanks not to Santa Claus, but to Baby Jesus (Ježíšek).

Chronology

895 > First recorded Přemyslid duke and first Christian ruler of Prague, Bořivoj, baptized by saints Cyril and Methodius.

929 > Prince Václav ("Good King Wenceslas") is martyred by his pagan brother Boleslav the Cruel.

973 > Under Boleslav the Pious, Prague becomes a bishopric.

1212 > Otakar I secures a royal title for himself and his descendants, who thereafter become kings of Bohemia.

1305 > Václav II dies heirless and the Přemyslid dynasty comes to an end.

1346–78 > During the reign of Holy Roman Emperor Charles IV, Prague enjoys its first Golden Age as the city is transformed by building projects into a fitting imperial capital.

1389 > Three thousand Jews slaughtered in the worst pogrom of the medieval period.

1415 > Czech religious reformer Jan Hus is found guilty of heresy and burnt at the stake in Konstanz (Constance).

1419 > Prague's first defenestration. Hus's followers, known as the Hussites, throw several councillors to their deaths from the windows of Prague's Nové Město's town hall.

1420 > Battle of Vítkov (a hill in Prague). Jan Žižka leads the Hussites to victory over the papal forces.

1434 > Battle of Lipany. The radical Hussites are defeated by an army of moderates and Catholics.

1526 > Habsburg rule in Prague begins, as Emperor Ferdinand I is elected King of Bohemia.

1576–1611 > Emperor Rudolf II establishes Prague as the royal seat of power, and ushers in the city's second Golden Age, summoning artists, astronomers and alchemists from all of Europe.

1618 > Prague's second defenestration. Two Catholic governors are thrown from the windows of Prague Castle by Bohemian Protestants. The Thirty Years' War begins.

1620 > Battle of the White Mountain, just outside Prague. The Protestants, under the "Winter King" Frederick of the Palatinate, are defeated by the Catholic forces; 27 Protestant nobles are executed on the Old Town Square.

1648 > The (Protestant) Swedes are defeated on Charles Bridge by Prague's Jewish and student populations. The Thirty Years' War ends.

1713 > Outbreak of the plague kills 13,000.

1757 > During the Seven Years' War, Prague is besieged and bombarded by the Prussians.

1781 > Edict of Tolerance issued by Emperor Joseph II, allowing a large degree of freedom of worship for the first time in 150 years.

1848 > Uprising in Prague eventually put down by Habsburg commander Alfred Prince Windischgätz. The ensuing reforms allow Jews to settle outside the ghetto for the first time.

1918 > The Habsburg Empire collapses due to defeat in World War I. Czechoslovakia founded.

1920 > Tomáš Masaryk elected as first president of Czechoslovakia.

1935 > Edvard Beneš elected as the second president of Czechoslovakia.

1938 > According to the Munich Agreement drawn up by Britain, France, Fascist Italy and Nazi Germany, the Czechs are forced to secede the border regions of the Sudetenland to Hitler.

1939 > In March, the Germans invade and occupy the rest of the Czech Lands. Slovakia declares independence.

1941 > Prague's Jews deported to Terezín (Theresienstadt) before being sent to the camps.

1942 > Nazi leader Reinhard Heydrich assassinated in Prague. The villages of Lidice and Ležáky are annihilated in retaliation.

1945 > On May 5, the Prague Uprising against the Nazis begins. On May 9, the Russians liberate the city. The city's ethnic German population is brutally expelled.

1946 > The Communist Party wins up to forty percent of the vote in first postwar general election. Beneš formally re-elected as president.

1948 > The Communist Party seizes power in a bloodless coup in February. Thousands flee the country. Jan Masaryk, Foreign Minister and son of the former president, dies in mysterious circumstances. Beneš resigns as president and is replaced by Communist leader, Klement Gottwald.

1952 > Twelve leading Party members (eleven of them Jewish) sentenced to death as traitors in Prague's infamous show trials.

1953 > Gottwald dies five days after Stalin.

1968 > During the "Prague Spring", reformers within the Party abolish censorship. Soviet troops invade the country and put a stop to the reform movement. Thousands go into exile.

1977 > 243 Czechs and Slovaks, including playwright Václav Havel, sign Charter 77 manifesto, reigniting the dissident movement.

1989 > After two weeks of popular protest, known as the Velvet Revolution, the Communist government resigns. Havel is elected as president.

1993 > Czechoslovakia splits into the Czech Republic and Slovakia. Havel is elected as Czech president.

1999 > The Czech Republic joins NATO.

2002 > In August, Prague is devastated by the worst floods in 200 years.

2003 > Václav Klaus is elected as the second Czech president.

2004 > The Czech Republic enters the European Union.

Czech

A modicum of English is spoken in Prague's central restaurants and hotels, and among the city's younger generation. Any attempt to speak Czech will be heartily appreciated, though don't be discouraged if people seem not to understand, as most will be unaccustomed to hearing foreigners stumble through their language. Unfortunately, Czech (**český**) is a highly complex western Slav tongue, into which you're unlikely to make much headway during a short stay.

Pronunciation

English-speakers often find Czech impossibly difficult to pronounce: just try the Czech tongue-twister, strč prst skrz krk (stick your finger down your neck). The good news is that, apart from a few special letters, each letter and syllable is pronounced as it's written – the trick is always to stress the first syllable of a word, no matter what its length; otherwise you'll render it unintelligible.

SHORT AND LONG VOWELS

Czech has both short and long vowels (the latter being denoted by a variety of accents):

a like the u in c**u**p
á as in f**a**ther
e as in p**e**t
é as in f**ai**r

ě like the ye in **ye**s
i or y as in p**i**t
í or ý as in s**ea**t
o as in n**o**t
ó as in d**oo**r
u like the oo in b**oo**k
ů or ú like the oo in f**oo**l

VOWEL COMBINATIONS AND DIPHTHONGS

There are very few diphthongs in Czech, so any combinations of vowels other than those below should be pronounced as two separate syllables.

au like the ou in f**ou**l
ou like the oe in f**oe**

CONSONANTS AND ACCENTS

There are no silent consonants, but it's worth remembering that r and l can form a syllable if standing between two other consonants or at the end of a word, as in Brno (Br-no) or Vltava (Vl-ta-va). The consonants listed below are those which differ substantially from the English. Accents look daunting, particularly the háček, which appears above c, d, l, n, r, s, t and z, but the only one which causes a lot of problems is ř, probably the most difficult letter to say in the entire language – even Czech toddlers have to be taught how to say it.

c like the **ts** in boats
č like the **ch** in chicken
ch like the **ch** in the Scottish loch
ď like the **d** in duped

The alphabet

In the Czech alphabet, letters which feature a **háček** (as in the č of the word itself) are considered separate letters and appear in Czech indexes immediately after their more familiar cousins. More confusingly, the consonant combination ch is also considered as a separate letter and appears in Czech indexes after the letter h.

g always as in goat, never as in general
h always as in have, but more energetic
j like the **y** in yoke
kd pronounced as **gd**
ľ like the **lli** in colliery
mě pronounced as mnye
ň like the **n** in nuance
p softer than the English **p**
r as in rip, but often rolled
ř like the sound of **r** and **ž** combined
š like the **sh** in shop
ť like the **t** in tutor
ž like the **s** in pleasure; at the end of a
   word like the **sh** in shop

Words and phrases

BASICS

Yes	ano
No	ne
Please/excuse me	prosím vás
Don't mention it	není zač
Sorry	pardon
Thank you	děkuju
Bon appétit	dobrou chuť
Bon voyage	šťstnou cestu
Hello/goodbye (informal)	ahoj
Hello (formal)	dobrý den
Goodbye (formal)	na shledanou
Good morning	dobré ráno
Good evening	dobrý večer
Good night (when leaving)	dobrou noc
How are you?	jak se máte?
I'm English/Irish /Scottish Welsh /American	ja jsem angličan(ka)// ir(ka)/skot(ka)/ velšan(ka)/ američan(ka)
Do you speak English?	mluvíte anglicky?
I don't speak German	nemluvím německy
I don't understand	nerozumím
I understand	rozumím
I don't know	nevím
Speak slowly	mluvíte pomalu
How do you say that in Czech?	jak se tohle řekne česky?
Could you write it down for me?	mužete mí to napsat?

Today	dnes
Yesterday	včera
Tomorrow	zítra
The day after tomorrow	pozítří
Now	hnet
Later	později
Wait a minute!	moment
Leave me alone!	dej mi pokoj!
Go away!	jdi pryč!
Help!	pomoc!
This one	tento
A little	trochu
Another one	ještě jedno -
Large/small	velký/malý
More/less	více/méně
Good/bad	dobrý/špatný
Cheap/expensive	levný/drahý
Hot/cold	horký/studený
With/without	s/bez
The bill please	zaplatím prosím
Do you have ...?	máte ...?
We don't have	nemáme
We do have	máme

QUESTIONS

What?	co?
Where?	kde?
When?	kdy?
Why?	proč?
Which one?	který/ktera?
This one?	ten/ta?
How many?	kolík?
What time does it open?	kdy máte otevřeno?
What time does it close?	kdy zavíráte?

GETTING AROUND

Over here	tady
Over there	tam
Left	nalevo
Right	napravo
Straight on	rovně
Where is ...?	kde je ...?
How do I get to Prague?	jak se dostanu do Prahy ?
How do I get to the...?	jak se dostanu k...?

By bus	autobusem
By train	vlakem
By car	autem
On foot	pěšky
By taxi	taxíkem
Stop here, please	zastavte tady, prosím
Ticket	jízdenka/lístek
Return ticket	zpáteční
Train station	nádraží
Bus station	autobusové nádraží
Bus stop	autobusová zastávka
When's the next train to Prague?	kdy jede další vlak do Prahy?
Is it going to Prague?	jede to do Prahy?
Do I have to change?	musím přestupovat?
Do I need a reservation?	musím mít místenku?
Is this seat free?	je tu volna?
May we (sit down)?	můžeme (se sednout)?

ACCOMMODATION

Are there any rooms available?	máte volné pokoje?
Do you have a double room?	máte jednou dvou lůžkovy pokoj?
For one night	na jednu noc
With shower	se sprchou
With bath	s koupelnou
How much is it?	kolík to stojí?
With breakfast?	se snídaně?

SOME SIGNS

Entrance	vchod
Exit	východ
Toilets	záchody/toalety
Men	muži
Women	ženy
Ladies	dámy
Gentlemen	pánové
Open	otevřeno
Closed	zavřeno
Pull/Push	sem/tam
Danger!	pozor!
Hospital	nemocnice
No smoking	kouření zakázáno
No entry	vstup zakázán

Arrival	příjezd
Departure	odjezd

DAYS OF THE WEEK

Monday	pondělí
Tuesday	uterý
Wednesday	středa
Thursday	čtvrtek
Friday	pátek
Saturday	sobota
Sunday	neděle
Day	den
Week	týden
Month	měsíc
Year	rok

MONTHS OF THE YEAR

Many Slav languages have their own highly individual systems in which the words for the names of the months are descriptive nouns, sometimes beautifully apt for the month in question.

January	leden (ice)
February	únor (hibernation)
March	březen (birch)
April	duben (oak)
May	květen (blossom)
June	červen (red)
July	červenec (redder)
August	srpen (sickle)
September	zaří (blazing)
October	říjen (rutting)
November	listopad (leaves falling)
December	prosinec (slaughter of pigs)

NUMBERS

1	jeden
2	dva
3	tří
4	čtyři
5	pět
6	šest
7	sedm
8	osm
9	devět
10	deset

11	jedenáct
12	dvanáct
13	třináct
14	čtrnáct
15	patnáct
16	šestnáct
17	sedmnáct
18	osmnáct
19	devatenáct
20	dvacet
21	dvacetjedna
30	třicet
40	čtyřicet
50	padesát
60	šedesát
70	sedmdesát
80	osmdesát
90	devadesát
100	sto
101	sto jedna
155	sto padesát pět
200	dvě stě
300	tři sta
400	čtyři sta
500	pět set
600	šest set
700	sedm set
800	osm set
900	devět set
1000	tisíc

Food and drink terms

BASICS

chléb	bread
chlebíček	(open) sandwich
cukr	sugar
hořčice	mustard
houska	round roll
knedlíky	dumplings
křen	horseradish
lžíce	spoon
maso	meat
máslo	butter
med	honey
mléko	milk
moučník	dessert
nápoje	drinks
na zdraví	cheers!
nůž	knife

oběd	lunch
obloha	garnish
ocet	vinegar
ovoce	fruit
pečivo	pastry
pepř	pepper
polévka	soup
předkrmy	starters
přílohy	side dishes
rohlík	finger roll
ryby	fish
rýže	rice
sklenice	glass
snídaně	breakfast
sůl	salt
šálek	cup
talíř	plate
tartarská omáčka	tartare sauce
večeře	supper/dinner
vejce	eggs
vidlička	fork
volské oko	fried egg
zeleniny	vegetables

COMMON TERMS

čerstvý	fresh
domácí	home-made
dušený	stew/casserole
grilovaný	roast on the spit
kyselý	sour
na kmíně	with caraway seeds
na roštu	grilled
nadívaný	stuffed
nakládaný	pickled
(za)pečený	baked/roast
plněný	stuffed
s.m. (s máslem)	with butter
sladký	sweet
slaný	salted
smažený	fried in breadcrumbs
studený	cold
syrový	raw
sýrový	cheesy
teplý	hot
uzený	smoked
vařený	boiled
znojmský	with gherkins

SOUPS

boršč	beetroot soup
bramborová	potato soup
čočková	lentil soup
fazolová	bean soup
hovězí vývar	beef broth
hrachová	pea soup
kapustnica	sauerkraut, mushroom and meat soup
kuřecí	thin chicken soup
rajská	tomato soup
zeleninová	vegetable soup

FISH

kapr	carp
losos	salmon
makrela	mackerel
platys	flounder
pstruh	trout
rybí filé	fillet of fish
sardinka	sardine
štika	pike
treska	cod
zavináč	herring/rollmop

MEAT DISHES

bažant	pheasant
biftek	beef steak
čevapčiči	spicy meat balls
dršt´ky	tripe
drůbež	poultry
guláš	goulash
hovězí	beef
husa	goose
játra	liver
jazyk	tongue
kachna	duck
klobásy	sausages
kotleta	cutlet
kuře	chicken
kýta	leg
ledvinky	kidneys
řízek	steak
roštěná	sirloin
salám	salami
sekaná	meat loaf
skopové maso	mutton

slanina	bacon
svíčková	fillet of beef
šunka	ham
telecí	veal
vepřový	pork
vepřové řízek	breaded pork cutlet or schnitzel
zajíc	hare
žebírko	ribs

VEGETABLES

brambory	potatoes
brokolice	broccoli
celer	celery
cibule	onion
česnek	garlic
chřest	asparagus
čočka	lentils
fazole	beans
houby	mushrooms
hranolky	chips, French fries
hrášek	peas
karot	carrot
květák	cauliflower
kyselá okurka	pickled gherkin
kyselé zelí	sauerkraut
lečo	ratatouille
lilek	aubergine
okurka	cucumber
pórek	leek
rajče	tomato
ředkev	radish
řepná bulva	beetroot
špenát	spinach
zelí	cabbage
žampiony	mushrooms

FRUIT, CHEESE AND NUTS

banán	banana
borůvky	blueberries
broskev	peach
brusinky	cranberries
bryndza	goat's cheese in brine
citrón	lemon
grejp	grapefruit
hermelín	Czech brie
hrozny	grapes

hruška	pear
jablko	apple
jahody	strawberries
kompot	stewed fruit
maliny	raspberries
mandle	almonds
meruňka	apricot
niva	semi-soft, crumbly, blue cheese
oříšky	peanuts
ostružiny	blackberries
oštěpek	heavily smoked, curd cheese
parenica	rolled strips of lightly smoked, curd cheese
pivní sýr	cheese flavoured with beer
pomeranč	orange
rozinky	raisins
švestky	plums
třešně	cherries
tvaroh	fresh curd cheese
urda	soft, fresh, whey cheese
uzený sýr	smoked cheese
vlašské ořechy	walnuts

DRINKS

čaj	tea
destiláty	spirits
káva	coffee
koňak	brandy
láhev	bottle
minerální (voda)	mineral (water)
mléko	milk
pivo	beer
presso	espresso
s ledem	with ice
soda	soda
suché víno	dry wine
šumivý	fizzy
svařené víno /svařák	mulled wine
tonic	tonic
vinný střik	white wine with soda
víno	wine

A glossary of Czech terms

brána	gate
český	Bohemian
chrám	large church
divadlo	theatre
dóm	cathedral
dům	house
hora	mountain
hospoda /hostinec	pub
hrad	castle
hřbitov	cemetery
kaple	chapel
katedrála	cathedral
kavárna	coffee house
klášter	monastery/convent
kostel	church
koupaliště	swimming pool
Labe	River Elbe
lanovka	funicular/cable car
les	forest
město	town
most	bridge
muzeum	museum
nábřeží	embankment
nádraží	train station
náměstí	square
ostrov	island
palác	palace
památník	memorial or monument
pasáž	shopping mall
pivnice	pub
radnice	town hall
restaurace	restaurant
sad	park
sál	room or hall
schody	steps
svatý/svatá	saint; often abbreviated to sv
třída	avenue
ulice	street
věž	tower
vinárna	wine bar or cellar
Vltava	River Moldau
vrchy	hills
výstava	exhibition
zahrada	garden
zámek	chateau

PUBLISHING INFORMATION

This first edition published January 2011 by **Rough Guides Ltd**

80 Strand, London WC2R 0RL

11, Community Centre, Panchsheel Park, New Delhi 110017, India

Distributed by the Penguin Group

Penguin Books Ltd, 80 Strand, London WC2R 0RL

Penguin Group (USA) 375 Hudson Street, NY 10014, USA

Penguin Group (Australia) 250 Camberwell Road, Camberwell, Victoria 3124, Australia

Penguin Group (NZ) 67 Apollo Drive, Mairangi Bay, Auckland 1310, New Zealand

This paperback edition published in Canada in 2010. Rough Guides is represented in Canada by Tourmaline Editions Inc., 662 King Street West, Suite 304, Toronto, Ontario, M5V 1M7

Typeset in Minion and Din to an original design by Henry Iles and Dan May.

Printed and bound in China

© Rob Humphreys 2011

Maps © Rough Guides

208pp includes index

A catalogue record for this book is available from the British Library

ISBN 978-1-8483-6599-5

3 5 7 9 8 6 4 2

MIX
Paper from responsible sources
FSC™ C018179
www.fsc.org

ROUGH GUIDES CREDITS

Text editor: Alice Park

Layout: Ankur Guha

Photography: Natascha Sturny, Dan Bannister and Eddie Gerald

Cartography: Katie Lloyd-Jones, Simonetta Giori

Picture editor: Sarah Cummins

Proofreader: Stewart Wild

Production: Rebecca Short

Cover design: Nicole Newman, Dan May and Chloë Roberts

THE AUTHOR

Rob Humphreys joined Rough Guides in 1989, having worked as a failed taxi driver and male model. He has travelled extensively in central and eastern Europe, writing guides to Vienna, the Czech and Slovak Republics, and St Petersburg, as well as London and Scotland.

ACKNOWLEDGEMENTS

Rob Humphreys would like to thank Kate for helping shepherd the numbs, and Josh and Rosie for investigating absinthe, and thanks to Alice for being brilliantly level-headed.

HELP US UPDATE

We've gone to a lot of effort to ensure that the first edition of the **Pocket Rough Guide Prague** is accurate and up-to-date. However, things change – places get "discovered", opening hours are notoriously fickle, restaurants and rooms raise prices or lower standards. If you feel we've got it wrong or left something out, we'd like to know, and if you can remember the address, the price, the hours, the phone number, so much the better.

Please send your comments with the subject line "**Pocket Rough Guide Prague Update**" to ⓔ mail@roughguides.com. We'll credit all contributions and send a copy of the next edition (or any other Rough Guide if you prefer) for the very best emails.

Find more travel information, connect with fellow travellers and book your trip on ⓦ www .roughguides.com

PHOTO CREDITS

All images © Rough Guides except the following:

Front cover Astronomical clock
© Humberto Olarte Cupas/Photolibrary
Back cover Tram on Mala Strana
© Eddie Gerald/Rough Guides
Title page Statues along the Charles Bridge
© Peter Adams/Corbis
p.4 Old Town Square © Robert Harding World Imagery/Corbis
p.5 View from Letná © Peter Erik Forsberg/ Alamy

p.25 Memorial of Jan Hus, Old Town Square
© GAPS photography/Arjan de Jager/iStock
p.29 Performance courtesy of Divadlo Archa
p.30 Stained glass, Obecní dům
© Christopher Kett/Alamy
p114 Olšany Cemetery © Shaun Higson Colour/Alamy

Index

Maps are marked in **bold**